PUZZLING

THEOLOGY

By

Rev. Douglas H. Ball, D.Min.

Chapter 1

A MASTERPIECE IS PAINTED

Is life just a constant struggle to live long enough to die?

Wouldn't a Creator have more in mind when this thing called existence was put together?

Let's surmise there was a Creator who decided to create all of existence, including us. If Creator planned it, I can picture Creator designing it all right down to every single individual Creator wanted in place in existence. And, for simplicity's sake, we will call Creator, God, and label God, Him. Let's also, for simplicity's sake, pretend He drew a likeness of every person that was to live in His existence, every likeness a framed work of art.

Let's picture them on His living room wall of His mansion, Heaven, the instant before He spoke His creation into being. Every family has a shelf or a wall that is the brag wall. You know the place where they hang or stand all the pictures of the kids and grandkids and maybe even some great-grandkids. I don't see them as spirit beings or anything, just paintings of the family, masterpieces of each and every one of the family that would ever be. God's mansion is infinite therefore He has room for billions of family pictures. Some brag wall, huh?

Did you catch that? We are a work of art, God's masterpiece.

So, what is a masterpiece? Looking into the source of the word we find that it comes from the ancient Greek word, *"poiema."* From this word we have the *poem* in English. While poem sounds very much like poiema, poiema denotes any quality work of art. We will use the painting of a portrait as our specific quality work of art in this discussion.

Each of us is the finest painting of *the* master painter of the universe. No finer artist has ever existed. He has painted His finest of masterpieces, one for each and every one of us. The Mona Lisa does not hold a candle to the beauty of the picture God has prepared for each of us. Let's get real personal, He has painted a beautiful picture of _____ (insert your name here).

Picture an awesome sunset, you are more beautiful. Picture the view across the Grand Canyon at sunrise on a stormy day, you are more beautiful. The master painter has made each of us more beautiful than these. Each in His image, yet each of these pictures is unique, different, one of a kind. There is none like me. There is none like you. While each is painted in the image of the Son of God, each is notably different from the one on the right and the left of yours.

✝ Think of the stories from Scripture you may have heard in Sunday School, Vacation Bible School, or maybe even from a Bible story book. Each one of them is different. The son didn't talk to the attacking Pharisees the same way he spoke to the rich young ruler who was, no doubt, also a Pharisee. Nor did he heal all the blind in the same way. One time he touched. Another time he made mud with spit and rubbed it on the blind man's eyes. One time the simple faith of touching a garment heals, while the next moment the person must be called forth out of the crowd. Sometimes he healed and then forgave sins, while the next he forgave first and then healed. Other times he healed without forgiving sins verbally. Each event, day and person brings us a different picture of the Son.

Did you realize that nowhere in Scripture do we have a physical description of the Son of God except one vague reference in Isaiah 53:2 which leads us to believe he is nothing special to look at? All of the other descriptions are heart, attitude, and action. Those are what God shows and looks for in us also, not skin color or hair length or even denomination of the church we are attending. I'd bet He will be something to look at when we get to see Him one of these days.

I used to tell my middle school students that they were all great actors who could portray many different people within themselves. They were one person when they were with other students of the same gender and another when they were with others of a different gender and another still when they were with a mixed group. They were also different with me, or when their mother, or when their father entered the room. They were someone else entirely when they were sent to the Principal's office on an errand than when they were sent because they were in trouble. They had no trouble with that teaching at all. In fact, many of them spent some time analyzing themselves as actors and the reason for the differences.

The Son shows himself to be different in varying circumstances while always remaining true to who He really is. His basic self was God and from that all else came. All the pictures we find in Scripture were Him without reservation. He was not acting, didn't use a different facade to fill each role. He was really himself in each and every case.

Our portrait is the same way. All the diverseness we will have is included in our portrait. Again, remember that all of us are unique, different from the same model. Have you ever taken an art class? Each student painting a picture of the apple, the orange and the flower in the vase that is sitting in the front of the room, but each portrayal comes out different in many small and big ways, but it is still the apple, the orange and the flower in the vase.

Only Creator knows how existence was to look, the fullness of the BIG PICTURE and therefore He is the only one who can give each one of us those certain characteristics in our portrait which will fill His role for us in this world. Because only He knows, we can never grasp the entirety of what is ourselves all by ourselves, let alone all that someone else might be in order to fulfill the BIG PICTURE, the eternal scheme of things. We have a hard time with just the picture of "eternal" let alone our own mortality.

To complicate the painting of these masterpieces even further we find from Scripture that these pictures are multi-dimensional. Many of the dimensions are also ones that we could put in a picture like length, width, and depth. We might even be able to handle time to a point. What about the dimensions of light or saltiness, we cannot handle that. And then there are the dimensions of Godliness, holiness, gifts and abilities.

One part of the painting we could handle easily is that the masterpieces for boys are blue and the masterpieces for girls are pink. Not really, that is just man's idea of distinction between the sexes. I thought I'd throw that in to see if you were paying attention.

Since these masterpieces of us are in God's living room, wouldn't it be great if God would have that picture out there ready for our parents and ourselves to see when we are first born? Just think as a parent for a moment. We would be able to know exactly which choices to make with each and every child in order for them to end up in the position God has painted for them from before the foundations of this world were ever set in place. We would know the classes for them to take and the special needs they would have. The talents that God had for them would be right out in the open and we could make sure they got the support they needed in those areas. The gifts they would eventually receive would also be known and it would be easy to facilitate all things for the entire future of that child. Somehow I think that would take all the wonder out of raising a child and turn it into a real job without joy or wonder.

Not having the picture before us is like the words of a college professor I once had. He said that we would only need 5% of what he was going to teach us throughout the semester, but he didn't know which 5% was needed by each of us so he had to teach us the whole enchilada so he would be sure we all got our needed 5%. And to think, I could have skipped 95% of his classes, but which 95%?

But, we do not have this picture that God has painted, it is hidden from us.

God has the picture. He has made the plans for each of us. We all have a niche in THE BIG PICTURE of the Creator. This picture which God has painted of each of us we just do not have. Finding this picture becomes very important, because it is the picture of all we could ever be. Not having it creates a constant struggle to find who we are and what we are here for. Could this search be what some folks call, "finding themselves?" After all, it is a search built into the spiritual DNA of each of us.

Man has philosophized for centuries about the reason for our existence. "What is life all about" and "why am I here," are constant questions. Just watch any teenager grow through the hormonal adjustments and you will see those two questions acted out on the broad stage of creation on a daily basis.

While we are looking for the masterpiece that is our life, let's begin at our beginning, the beginning of us as we know us, birth. We could go back to conception, the beginning of life, but that would stretch the imagination just a bit too far.

When we are born our future is like a puzzle, just a bunch of pieces of varying shape, size, pattern, color, complexity, and number in a box. That is our masterpiece painted by God before the world began.

Whoa! What happened to that beautiful, beyond words portrait hanging on the wall of God's living room?

God has rules in His creation. The planets follow rules,

paths. The stars are in their private places and move according to rules. We have rules. The first man created had one rule. He was not to do something. He went and did it anyhow. There was only one rule and he blew it. We can get into deep discussion on this passage, but the bottom line is that first man did what God told him not to. That original sin (not following Creator's rules) has been in our genes ever since because we are the descendants of first man and first woman, everyone one of us. Hey, sister, how you doing? Howdy, bro.

And, then, Creator took the pictures off the wall of His living room and cut them into little pieces. He didn't throw them away. He didn't throw Adam and Eve away. He gave them a chance at putting their pictures back together again, but they had to figure it out for themselves even though God would provide the way and the clues. They started the big questions of "Who am I?" and "Why am I here?" and had to look for the clues that God provided in His creation.

Chapter 2

A REAL MESS TO CLEAN UP

There we are a bunch of pieces comfy in a non-descript cardboard box when, BLAM, the box gets slammed by a tremendous force; the box comes totally unglued and the pieces are scattered all over the place. We have just purposely and with malice aforethought sinned all on our own. We can no longer blame our predicament on Adam and Eve, and their sin, or anyone else. It has now gotten very personal. We have chosen to disobey one or more of Creator's rules. It is our sin, our life, our puzzle, and our box is destroyed.

We have no one to blame but ourselves for the mess we are now in. Before, we could have blamed us being in a mess of pieces in a non-descript box on Adam or Eve, but now it is our fault and our condition is even more precarious.

At birth there was hope. The pieces were all together, but with personal sin (missing the perfection that God had in mind for us when He first painted our portrait) the pieces are literally scattered beyond earthly hope. When there is no hope, there is no purpose to life. Only in hope do we find purpose.

Each of the pieces that is a part of our puzzle is now scattered and even worse, held far apart by the sin in our lives. Between every possible connection of those pieces is sin blocking the joint. God tells us that all men sin and don't live up to what He had planned for them. (Romans 3:23) The choices we make on a daily, even moment by moment, basis keep us apart from all that God wanted for us to be and to have, and separates us from the God that created us to begin with. Much the same as if we were kicked out of the family home for some terrible reason, we are just a scattered shambles of lost, without meaning, without hope puzzle pieces. We can never be the person that God intended for us to be without being able to find and connect all the pieces. We just have to get ourselves together.

Some of the pieces, maybe even a majority of them, are close to home. Some of them are a bit farther away, out of sight. Then there are those that landed in other people's pockets. And, there are those that ended up in China, or Korea, or Africa, or Lower Slobovia. So far apart are the pieces of us that not only can we not see them, but we have no idea where to look. We have no idea of what the picture looks like, where the pieces are, or even how many of them there are. Many are just plain totally beyond our vision and horizons.

Interesting word, "horizons." It comes from the Greek *horizo*. This can mean horizon or limits. It also means "boundaries."

What are your boundaries at this point? Do you have limits? Is the horizon your limit? Buzz Lightyear isn't held by limits, his goal is "to infinity and beyond." That's pretty limitless. How about you?

At this point you just don't know, do you?

Once upon a time I was a sailor, bell bottom trousers and Dixie-cup hat. During much of that time it was my pleasure to be an instructor. I found that there were three types of sailors in my classes. One didn't fit any molds; they were a very, very small group so we'll forget about them for the purposes of this discussion. The second type was city boys. The third was country boys.

I found that the city boys had no idea of their limits. After much thought I realized they had never been tested in a way that would allow them to find those limits. I have never been sure of the reason, but I suspect it has to do with having other folks around all the time to call upon and their horizons were very close. They were inconsistent. The city boys rarely got anywhere near the same grades week after week on exams, nor did they have the confidence to wade into unknown waters without serious consideration.

The country boys seemed to know who they were and what their limits were. I surmised that working alone and with varying types of equipment and critters taught them just what they could handle and what they could not. They loved new challenges and met them head on. They tended to get very close to the same grades each week. They tended to be very consistent and confident in performance, not in a rut, but their horizons were much further out.

Because of this, I chose to move to the country to raise my kids after I got out of the Navy. I wanted my kids to have far horizons, limits, boundaries.

What do you see when you look at your horizons? Is there a confidence that you can handle whatever comes along and make it work for you? You know, like a sixteen year old that has all the answers, but has yet to learn the real questions.

I don't know about you, but when I put a puzzle together I start with the edges, the limits. Once the edges are complete and the corners are firmly in place there is a real feel for the complexity of the puzzle, its size, and how the colors and edges match the picture on the box. Proceeding is then possible no matter how complex the puzzle is.

So, how do we put our puzzle together without having any horizons (the edges), or picture, or all the pieces, or even the foggiest idea of what it will look like in the end? Much like a nineteen year old who finally realizes the questions she held in her mind were not the questions that really had meaning in her life. Where do I go from here?

To further complicate matters all of your masterpiece

pieces are mixed with the pieces to all the other lives around you that haven't yet been plugged into masterpieces and many are stored in some garage someplace (more on that later).

Okay, let's really get the picture. In order to get the picture of what things look like at this point, go to that closet where you store all the old puzzles, adults' and kids' puzzles, and take down the whole stack. Gather the stacks from all the other closets. Borrow the neighbor's puzzles. You might want to tell them they probably won't get them back anytime soon, if ever. Don't forget the neighbor on the other side or the ones across the street. Open each one of those puzzles and dump the contents into a pile in the middle of the street in front of your house. Invite your neighbors to join you in this exercise, they'll enjoy it and maybe even learn something. Oh yeah, make sure it is a really windy day and a busy street. Now, grab huge hands full of the pile of pieces and throw them up in the air, sideways, front ways and all ways you can. Throw them on passing cars. Get some on the semi as it passes, that container may be headed for Hawaii. Look around you. What a mess you have made of those puzzles! But, wasn't it fun?

That's what a masterpiece separated by sin looks like. As we sin we make the same type of mess with our lives. The God given plan is scattered and shattered in all directions rather than in the pattern that God had intended. It happened to Adam and Eve and it happens to us, all because of sin.

So what is this sin that tears our masterpiece limb from limb, piece from piece? The Word of God says sin is all unrighteousness. Righteousness is what God wants and unrighteousness is what He does not want. How do we find out what God wants? Read His Word. Learn of Him. Prayer helps in many ways. Jesus boiled it all down to two rules when asked by the legal beagles of His day, "What is the greatest commandment of God?"

Jesus replied, "Love God with all you are and then there is a second which goes with the first so tightly they cannot be separated, love everybody else." (Matthew 22:27-30)

Simple, huh?

All we have to do is love God and everybody else. Unfortunately, I don't believe you can do that until you realize just how much God loves you and surrender to that love. So there we are scattered all over the place in sin.

But, wait, there is hope. If we dig deep into our pockets (you might call it your inner being) we will each find one little piece that landed there.

If you are smart, you quickly realize that you can no more put together the puzzle that is you with one piece than an anthropologist can put a society together with all its habits, diet and religion, even the dress and habitations, from one little piece of bone no matter what part of the body that bone came from. You may try to, but it just does not contain all the information needed to complete the entire picture, just as a scrap of bone does not give us anywhere near the entire picture of a person. Hints, yes. More information than we may have had before, yes, but nothing even close to the entire picture by any means.

All this reminds me of the blind men describing an elephant. One grabs the tail and states that an elephant is like a rope. Another grabs the trunk and describes an elephant as a huge hose. Still another grabs an ear and uses the term, leathery wings. The last feels a leg and says an elephant is like a tree. All true, but none of them described the big picture or even came close to a real understanding of the total elephant.

But wait! There's more. Don't throw that one piece away. It, like the descriptions of the blind men and the bone of the anthropologist, is a clue to the complete picture.

You can count on it not being a corner or even an edge, matter of fact; the odds are completely against it. It will probably be a non-descript piece of blue that could come from the sky in the background of our masterpiece or is it the stream or ocean, maybe even an eye or boat or the dress on a charming lady that will be or is a serious part of your life. Then again, it could be something you cannot even think of in your wildest dreams. Not knowing what the picture will be, color just doesn't help. We will call that piece your spirit. Hold on to that piece for dear life and contemplate it from time to time.

Chapter 3

WANDERING AND WONDERING

We take our one piece everywhere we go looking for purpose in that one piece. We may even grab a puzzle piece off the ground as we walk looking for purpose and then try to fit it to the one piece we have. We may look to nature to provide answers or even a circle of rocks for the power to put us together. Most of us spend much of our lives, maybe even all of our lives, wandering around wondering what the picture would be like, while exerting absolutely no effort at all to get it put together. What a pity!

We just never get around to picking up the pieces of our lives.

How many times have you heard the idea expressed, "I am just going to find myself?"

I have heard that many times. There was a boss of mine in the Navy that came back off of an extended submarine patrol only to have his wife hand him the kids and say, "I'm going out looking for who I really am. I'll be back when I get back - after I find myself." She never came back. I can only assume she never found herself. My boss was personified in the country western song, "No news." She was personified by unhappiness and loneliness, totally unfulfilled by anything.

There are so many places to look and without guidance we end up like Solomon the wise king of Israel. (Although I wonder how wise a man can be who has a thousand wives.

That doesn't spell wisdom in my book. One is great. {I had to say that, my wife is editing this for me.})

God at one point was so impressed with Solomon that He granted Solomon one wish, any wish he wanted. Solomon thought about it for about 2 seconds and asked to be wise so he could rule Israel properly. God was so impressed with Solomon that He not only granted that wish, but made him the richest king of the richest nation on earth at the time. You can read about it in 1 Kings 3.

We are not all as fortunate as Solomon. His father, David, had ruled Israel for 40 years or so and had whupped all the neighbors into submission and had them paying tribute when he died, leaving Solomon a peaceful, rich nation. Solomon then proceeded to make Israel even richer and more stable by marrying a bunch of princesses from surrounding countries which is how he got many of the wives.

The custom of the day was for a daughter to be given to the more powerful king by the weaker or defeated king to seal a treaty. Sometimes the princes of a defeated king were taken and made eunuch servants of the winning king, but we won't talk about that part.

So here's Solomon; rich, famous, and wiser than anybody else, and he, too, has a puzzle to put together. After all, he is only human. You might ask, "With all the money and all the wisdom, how tough can that be?" He could even have hired master puzzle completers, valedictorians of the renowned International School of Puzzling.

Solomon goes out to get it all together, to find himself, to answer the age old question, "Who am I and why am I here?" He is also looking for some pleasure in life, you know, the warm fuzzies we all want, and the fun and excitement of life, the gusto.

I said to myself, "Come now, be merry; enjoy yourself to the full." But I found that this, too, was futile. For it is silly to be laughing all the time; what good does it do?

So after a lot of thinking, I decided to try the road of drink, while still holding steadily to my course of seeking wisdom.

Next I changed my course again and followed the path of folly, so that I could experience the only happiness most men have throughout their lives.

Then I tried to find fulfillment by inaugurating a great public works program: homes, vineyards, gardens, parks, and orchards for myself, and reservoirs to hold the water to irrigate my plantations.

Next I bought slaves, both men and women, and others were born within my household. I also bred great herds and flocks, more than any of the kings before me. I collected silver and gold as taxes from many kings and provinces.

In the cultural arts, I organized men's and women's choirs and orchestras.

And then there were my many beautiful concubines.

So I became greater than any of the kings in Jerusalem before me, and with it all I remained clear-eyed, so that I could evaluate all these things. Anything I wanted I took and did not restrain myself from any joy. I even found great pleasure in hard work. This pleasure was, indeed, my only reward for all my labors.

But as I looked at everything I had tried, it was all so useless, a chasing of the wind, and there was nothing really worthwhile anywhere.

Now I began a study of the comparative virtues of wisdom and folly, and anyone else would come to the same conclusion I did, that wisdom is of more value than foolishness, just as light is better than darkness; for the wise man sees, while the fool is blind. And yet I noticed that there was one thing that happened to wise and foolish alike just as the fool will die, so will I. So of what value is all my wisdom? Then I realized that even wisdom is futile. For the wise and fool both die, and in the days to come both will be long forgotten. So now I hate life because it is all so irrational; all is foolishness, chasing the wind.

And I am disgusted about this-that I must leave the fruits of all my hard work to others. (Ecclesiastes 2:1-18)

Did you catch all of that? First Solomon tries laughter: bring on the clowns. That didn't work. Then booze enters the picture and then folly (wine, women and song), those didn't work, either. After those, he gets into the work of building parks and playgrounds, great opera houses and building up great houses and estates for himself; even a bit of charity work was attempted. Buying slaves wouldn't work. Herds and flocks, no matter how large, didn't work. Being richer (How do you get richer than richest?) didn't help at all. Nothing material gave the slightest satisfaction or sense of completion.

Finally, he gets close. He goes after wisdom. This only brought him to the conclusion that all people, rich or poor, wise or stupid, die. This, too, was not the way for him to find himself and get it all together. He found it all to be just so much hot air, smoke, or emptiness.

In the end of his train of thought and action (at least he was acting instead of warming a recliner), Solomon comes to the idea that it is all a waste of time trying to get it all together of his own accord because he is only going to die and leave it all to someone else. Yep, you just rack up all the stuff and then you die, leaving it to the kids and relatives, with the government getting a big chunk of it first. He who dies with the most toys is still dead. Talk about fatalistic, he's got the attitude.

But, look around you. Check the mirror. Is that your attitude also?

It is?

When you have "Born to Die" tattooed on your attitude you reflect the problem here. There must be a bigger reason for existence than just dying, even Solomon picked up on that. By the way, I dreamed of a gal once who worked in a fabric factory and had "Born to Dye" tattooed on her left shoulder, but that's a different story altogether.

What do we do to change things? We have tripped over the prime paradigm of Madison Avenue.

I don't know why we say that advertising is Madison Avenue, or comes from there, or is there, or whatever. I heard once that it was the address of major advertising firms and that's how advertising came to be called Madison Avenue. Oh well, enough of that.

Madison Avenue counts on people trying to pick up the pieces and get it all together. They count on them realizing something is missing. The advertiser's formula is to convince folks that they, the product makers, have the one missing piece that cannot be lived without, the one that will make them complete and fulfilled, thereby causing them to run right out and buy their product no matter the cost or how much further in debt it will put them. This new piece will make them deliriously happy and they will never desire for anything ever again.

They have so completely imprinted your need for this product on your mind that you run out and buy this piece, only to find that it partially satisfies for a while and then you realize that something is still missing in your life. Your disappointment again abounds and you begin looking for the next real thing which will fill all the voids in your life only to be sold another bill of goods of little or no real value. Buying a certain car will not make you look any better than you look now. The other brand of makeup won't either. All the lotion in the world will not keep you from dying. You can eat all that cereal they will ever make and not be a champion. That mighty midget doll will not fly across the room under its own power and crash a hole in the wall so you can escape from your bedroom.

You have come to the bottom of the problem, you cannot live, be truly alive, with pieces of you all over the world (remember those on the semi or caught by the wind?). At this point you look for pieces in a very serious way. You will leave no piece unturned, untried, unexamined in order to get yourself together.

Chapter 4

ALL THE PRETTY PIECES

Something new now hits you with a smack of pain. Look at all the pretty pieces scattered everywhere you go. There are simple, single pieces in flat earth tones, others with intricate designs that catch your eye and there are even ones with gold and silver, jewels and fancy geegaws you have always wanted. There are so many of them that you are greatly confused.

"Can they all be parts of me?" you ask yourself.

Thinking only of yourself, you begin to pick up all the pieces that catch your eye. The one stacked high with glittering gold. There's one with a Ferrari on it. How about the one with the big house or even that high paying job? Don't forget that one with the college education at a prestigious university. There are also the pieces with booze and/or drugs just for you. You grab and grab. You buy tickets to the "Pieces Lottery" which will supply you with millions of pieces when you win. Of course, that thinking is just Madison Avenue all over again.

Pretty soon your pockets are full. The garage is full. The spare room is full. Every space you have is full of pieces, all pretty, but useless because they just don't fit together. Wait a minute here's a couple that go together and here's a couple more over here. Hope springs eternal in the breast of man. At this point you remind me of the brother in the movie "Second Hand Lions" who has just sold his brother to the evil sheik and is so burdened with the gold he can hardly walk. He is now rich beyond his wildest dreams, but can hardly walk. Later he just sits on the front porch doing nothing but existing with all that wealth, the pieces neatly stacked, hidden from the rest of the world.

But, what do you do with all of these pieces that are burdening you, the ones taking up so much space and confusing the living daylights out of you? They are even causing you to fret and become neurotic with the ideas of what might be and/or even wracked with fear over who is trying to steal them. Possessing and protecting quickly become overpowering ideas for you.

You rent a secure storage locker or build another garage.

One of the fastest growing small businesses in the United States is storage places. Storage for our stuff (pieces), our RV's, our boats, our mink coats, our important papers, the old flatware, the high school face books, and all the other stuff we accumulate. In my little town of 3,500 folks there are 3 storage facilities with a fourth one being built on the main drag.

I think of King Saul hunting David. Saul lies down amongst his *stuff* to sleep. Why is he amongst the stuff? Could it be that he just has to protect all he owns and drags along with him and who better to do it than himself? Or, perhaps he feels safe and comfortable amongst all these familiar items. Jesus said that the rich man spent his life worrying about his stuff so much that he had no time for anything else (Matthew 6:24). And then he added that it is more difficult for a rich man to enter the kingdom of God than for a camel to go through the eye of a needle (Matthew 19:24)

Those with a lot of pieces put themselves in jeopardy. The more you have the more others want it. At least that is what goes through the mind of a person with lots of stuff. Saul almost got killed amongst his stuff. David and his buddy sneaked up on Saul and the buddy was willing and begging to do Saul in by pinning Him to the ground with his spear.

David stopped him.

I haven't figured how to get a camel through the eye of a needle yet, either. There is hope. Jesus said right after that statement that through Him all things are possible (Matthew 19:26), the Creator of the universe knows what is needed to get that camel anywhere He wants that camel to be and He can do it without breaking a sweat.

There must be a way to get all these pieces in their proper place and build the glorious life masterpiece that God has prepared for us. HE never tells us to do what we cannot do, nor what He has not already exemplified for us in the life of His Son, Jesus the Christ, to show us the way.

Do we keep all these pretty pieces that may or may not have any value for us, or what? How do we know if they are our pieces? Could it be that we are each thinking, "finders, keepers?"

Realizing that some of these pieces must belong to someone else we begin to look around at others. Once again we find that because of the burden of pieces we have in our possession we cannot see beyond ourselves. Our view is totally blocked by our collection of pieces and our overpowering desire to collect more. Between possessing, protecting and prospecting for more, our life is totally consumed. It quickly becomes all about me, myself, and mine.

This thinking leads to many addictions. We are looking for all the pleasure we can give ourselves that our focus is so warped by the addiction of self that we can go nowhere except down. These addictions can be so bad that moms trade their children for them and dads walk away from all their responsibilities in the home. Some of each just plain go to jail, not collecting $200, just losing all they have because of the addiction. I have no idea how many families have been destroyed, how many lives have been destroyed, or how many are currently being destroyed by the addictions of one or more members of the family.

Craig Groeschel in his book *"Weird"* states:

"We're afraid," my counselor continued, "That if we don't just run nonstop and try everything this world has to offer, we're going to miss out on something. We're afraid that we might miss that one thing that turns out to be that one elusive piece of our puzzle that will finally fill the void we feel so deeply. But nothing can. There's no such thing as a healthy addiction." (Page 52)

Most folks collect. Look around you. How many collections do you have? The old music tapes, the stamps, coins, tea pots, salt shakers, whatever; most people have a collection of something. My son has a collection of sports cards. It used to be very important to him and he spent lots of his money on more cards. Today it is sitting in his closet collecting dust, but someday it may be worth something, at least that is his hope.

Let's back up a bit. Many people never realize that some of these pieces might never be theirs. They continue to collect and hoard. After all, they might be worth something someday. They continue to grab them up indiscriminately and stash them in hidey holes where they think no one can find them. They never find the Master Painter's plan for their lives because they are buried in pieces of what they see as the good life and cannot see THE best life. Kind of like the old saying, "You can't see the forest for the trees."

Do we ever get to the point where we have it all and don't know what to do with it, whatever IT is? (Or, at least we think we have it all.) Nah! When someone asks how many is enough, we respond, "Just one more."

How sad to think you could have it all and not know it or what to do with it! So, we keep on searching for just that one more piece that just may be the key to it all and bring us real happiness and fulfillment.

Many folks at this point begin searching for someone or something to put our masterpiece together, or at least teach them how to put it together.

Chapter 5

OUR "HIGHER POWER" ENTERS THE PICTURE

We realize our lives are totally out of control and scream for a "higher power," a god, to take control of the pieces and put them together in some semblance of order.

This "higher power" idea comes from Alcoholics Anonymous. The above paragraph is a paraphrase of the third step of the twelve steps of AA.

I have a friend, Dan, whose higher power for a while was a boulder, a large boulder the size of a house out in the woods of Wisconsin. When he needed to discuss his addictions with his higher power he would go into the woods and sit at the bottom of this boulder with his back to it and discuss his life and the process of recovery from his addictions with the boulder. It worked for him for a little while.

Dan told me of a friend of his in AA whose higher power was his Harley. When the pieces of life stacked up too high to see around or over, he would get on his Harley and ride. He stated that anyplace his Harley couldn't get him wasn't a place he wanted to be anyhow.

So, what's your "higher power," your god?

In AA you now surrender the job of getting you together or at least teaching you how to get it together to whatever or whoever that higher power is. The strange part at this point is that most folks aren't going to surrender to anything. They cry out, "I am in charge. I am the ruler of my own life and nothing is going to circumvent that idea. After all, what higher power can there be than I? There can be nothing more interested, concerned, or focused on me other than me, so it is up to me alone to make me all I can be."

"But, I am really confused by all the pieces."

We realize somewhere along the line of life that we need something or someone stronger than ourselves to help, if only long enough to get started getting us put together.

We become surrendered to a "higher power" only to the extent that we will listen to a higher power without trying to be the higher power ourselves. Or, we will choose what suggestions our "higher power" has that we like and want to do or be, rejecting all others. We design our own "higher power" one step at a time.

As we watch the pieces going into place we don't like that section or this color scheme over here. The whole thing just isn't very aesthetically pleasing to our eyes and we just take charge again in putting us together.

We have reached out to some "higher power" to put us together and find that we are not satisfied with that "higher power" as a construction contractor for our lives. That's a simple problem, we throw out the old and find another "higher power" or we design another "higher power" which fits our needs at the time and is more to our own liking. Personally designed "higher powers" are like so much smoke. Impressive to look at for a while, but valueless, dissipating quickly into the emptiness that it really is. The great thing about them is the ability to understand them because they are us, designed by us, in our own image for our own purposes and aggrandizement.

Every time our "higher power" does something we don't like or want to do, we alter our "higher power" until we come up with one that is made in "our own image." We now have a designer "higher power." Many folks seriously mistake the designer "higher power" for the real thing, or they even begin collecting designer higher powers and hoarding them which begins another endless cycle of collecting confusion. Which one do I use at this time for this problem with these people, confusing the issue even further.

And, what a wonderful god it is, too. It must be real. It looks like us and smells like us, and has the same power as us. Our god has become us. "I am my own god" is the realization when you look in the mirror and then at the picture of a "higher power" god you have painted in order to get yourself together. You have found yourself as you would put you together, not how the Creator God wanted you.

How much help can that "higher power" god be? You are right back where you started, with you trying to put you together with all the pieces you have collected and stored in all those places. Now you have a collection of partially completed puzzles put together by your totally useless collection of designer higher powers, which are not stronger, wiser, more knowledgeable, or compassionate than you. They even have the same prejudices and outlook as you.

WHOOPEE!

The ultimate mistake in our lives is to paint our own picture of God or ourselves.

13 You made all the delicate, inner parts of my body and knit them together in my mother's womb.

14 Thank you for making me so wonderfully complex! It is amazing to think about. Your workmanship is marvelous-and how well I know it.

15 You were there while I was being formed in utter seclusion!

16 You saw me before I was born and scheduled each day of my life before I began to breathe. Every day was recorded in your book! TLB (Psalm 139:13-16)

and

11 For I know the thoughts that I think toward you, saith the LORD, thoughts of peace, and not of evil, to give you an expected end. KJV (Jeremiah 29:11)

These two passages of Scripture tell us of God's original plan for us, each of them points to a complexity and beauty that we can never know without him. This Creator God has also given us a true picture of Himself and for us to change that picture is to change the very nature of the Creator God into a *designer god* which has no more ability or power than we have. Designer clothes may make us look wonderful, beautiful and fashionable in the world's eyes, but designer gods do nothing except confuse the idea of the real Creator God. They will never make us all that the Creator has desired of us when He painted the Masterpiece we want to get together, which brings us to designer selves, us painting our own masterpiece. That won't work either, for the same reasons.

I mean, come on, some lizard in a commercial says that this company is so nice that they will give you an English muffin with butter and jam, and then they must state a disclaimer for fear someone will believe the stupidity of the commercial advertisement and then find it is a lie. Then these gullible folks will sue the company that doesn't give a disclaimer of the lie that is so fantastic no sane person would believe it anyhow. Then there is the question of a talking lizard convincing folks to buy a product anyhow. If the lizard is a fantasy, what does that say for the product being sold? Could it be we have grown so used to the fantasies that we are ignoring the realities? Yeah, I know it is a gecko and having lived in places where geckos hang from the ceiling chittering all the time I can tell you they are not cute and they are not to be trusted. They will lay eggs and poop in your light switch boxes and wall outlets, even in the corners of the rooms. They will also fall off the ceiling into the bathtub (personal experience for my wife, quite the excitement).

Would you really put yourself in the hands of a Harley or a boulder the size of a house? A boulder cannot even talk to you, although it may provide a bit of solidarity to your life. While a Harley can make lots and lots of noise, is there value in that noise beyond the indication of power? It may take you off this earth for a moment, but the landing could be something less than what you are looking for. And, do you really trust a lizard whose ultimate goal is an English muffin with butter and jam?

We cannot find ourselves in the pieces available no matter what the boulder, Harley or the lizard says. Are we so gullible that we think we can create god in our own image? If so, we are in trouble. The pieces will never go together as the Masterpiece the Creator has painted from before the foundations of creation.

We haven't found Him, yet.

Chapter 6

THE HIGHEST POWER

Remember the statement you threw out in conversations to make yourself sound really intelligent (maybe you didn't, but I did and so did all the wanna-be intelligentsia of my sixth grade class) which went something like, "If you put an infinite number of monkeys on an infinite number of typewriters (or computers with word processing software nowadays) and give them an infinite amount of time, the greatest book of all time would be written." Come on! That's just like believing that given nothing everything can be made by accident; or, to restate, given an infinite amount of nothing and an infinite amount of time, everything will appear. How about, given an indefinite number of pieces and a finite brain, you can make something of yourself.

Does that sound true to you?

Didn't think so.

The end of this is that given an infinite amount of nothing and an infinite amount of time, nothing will appear, unless of course you are the God of Creation.

We go back to our first verse, the very first verse, *"In the beginning, God created the heavens and the earth."* (Genesis 1:1) The fancy term is Ex Nihil, which means "out of nothing." In the very beginning of everything except God, God was and created everything out of nothing, because nothing existed at that point except God and He, according to Scripture is Spirit, not mass. Therefore, nothing existed except one Spirit, in three persons.

Leo Tolstoy states in his book, <u>A Confession</u>, "You are an accidentally united lump of something." He doesn't discuss where that something came from and what caused it to get together and become you or me or them.

Are we just an accident?

I don't think so!

I have heard from a couple of sources that there are nearly 300 theories as to the origins of everything and all but 2 of them require a prime mover, a force, a Creator to at least get the process started. Remember that one of the basic laws of physics is that an object at rest remains at rest until acted upon by an outside force. What or who is that outside force of creation quickly becomes *the* question? Another law to think on is the law of conservation of mass and energy. This law states that the amount of mass and energy in the universe remains constant. Where did the first mass and energy come from?

Perhaps it was a Big Bang. Who put the mass in place to go bang? Who caused the bang? Where did the energy come from?

Then there is the idea that Hydrogen came together and that the clustering (was that fusion?) of Hydrogen atoms brought into being all the other elements. Who made the first Hydrogen? Or, where did the first proton, neutron, or electron come from? Was all this just some kind of cosmic accident that somehow was able to circumvent all the laws of physics and matter as we know them today? Do you see how easy it is to get to the idea of a Creator?

I still like the Big Bang idea myself. I can only imagine, after all it cannot be replicated in a laboratory, that when God spoke and all the worlds, heavens, stars, comets and earth sprang into being out of nothing, there was an awfully large

BANG!

It didn't happen by accident, it was planned. It didn't cause itself to be created or create itself. A Creator caused it and, if there were anyone around to hear it, it was the most fantastic bang of undoubtedly infinite proportions. Science says it is still going on and can still be heard. It must have been some noisy party.

To look back at our analogy of the masterpiece that is you, we must realize that there must have been a creator of the canvas, the pigments, the brushes, all the requirements of a masterpiece outside of talent. Without all the components and a force to move them into place those masterpieces would never have been brought into being to begin with.

As you walk through the Louvre in Paris, a local art gallery, or WalMart looking at the framed art, did it ever cross your mind that these masterpieces came together accidentally out of nothing? Me neither. The talent of the painter is what always comes to mind, which, in our case, is the Creator of the universe and us.

As we established in chapter one, God created all the masterpieces that are now puzzles whose pieces are scattered all over the place, just as He created all that is everything. He is the only one who has seen the masterpiece that is you. He is the only one who can recreate the masterpiece just exactly the way He designed and intended for you to be.

You can, "CAN," (God allows choices, even wrong ones) call on anyone you want to put together the pieces you have collected. You can call upon your designer god (discussed in the last chapter). There are many folks who think that the answer resides within themselves and all they have to do is bring it out through the power of the god that is them. There are even others who claim to have established something which just might be you, such as the Buddha or Allah or

Krishna or even the one eyed god in the corner of the den or living room, but there is only one Creator of the universe and all the masterpieces that are mankind, and that is the God of Creation.

Chapter 7

STRANGE PICTURES

Because we can get anyone or anything to attempt to put together the puzzle that is us, perhaps it will do us some good to look at a couple of masterpieces not put together by the Creator who originated them and see what happened.

The first is in the Bible in John 4, verses 4-18:

4 And he must needs go through Samaria.

5 Then cometh he to a city of Samaria, which is called Sychar, near to the parcel of ground that Jacob gave to his son Joseph.

6 Now Jacob's well was there. Jesus therefore, being wearied with his journey, sat thus on the well: and it was about the sixth hour.

7 There cometh a woman of Samaria to draw water: Jesus saith unto her, Give me to drink.

8(For his disciples were gone away unto the city to buy meat.)

9 Then saith the woman of Samaria unto him, How is it that thou, being a Jew, askest drink of me, which am a woman of Samaria? for the Jews have no dealings with the Samaritans.

10 Jesus answered and said unto her, If thou knewest the gift of God, and who it is that saith to thee, Give me to drink; thou wouldest have asked of him, and he would have given thee living water.

11 The woman saith unto him, Sir, thou hast nothing to draw with, and the well is deep: from whence then hast thou that living water?

12 Art thou greater than our father Jacob, which gave us the well, and drank thereof himself, and his children, and his cattle?

13 Jesus answered and said unto her, Whosoever drinketh of this water shall thirst again:

14 But whosoever drinketh of the water that I shall give him shall never thirst; but the water that I shall give him shall be in him a well of water springing up into everlasting life.

15 The woman saith unto him, Sir, give me this water, that I thirst not, neither come hither to draw.

16 Jesus saith unto her, Go, call thy husband, and come hither.

17 The woman answered and said, I have no husband. Jesus said unto her, Thou hast well said, I have no husband:

18 For thou hast had five husbands; and he whom thou now hast is not thy husband: in that saidst thou truly. KJV

In this story we have a woman who is so messed up that she must sneak out in the heat of the day (the sixth hour, noon) to draw water. Most folks in town are taking a siesta at that time. What is going on? We don't find out until verse 18. She has had five husbands (any relation to some folks on the society pages?) and the man she is now living with is not her husband, he is some other woman's husband. There is no happiness or joy, only hiding from the other women of the town so she will not be stoned to death or beaten up by the irate wife.

She has been putting her own masterpiece together all by herself for years. She has determined up to this point to be her own god, make her own rules regardless of what others say, and create herself in her own image of herself. Doesn't look to me like it is working too well, unless she wants a trail of broken relationships strung out behind her and assuming she likes sneaking around in the heat of the day doing her household chores because the others she has to live in close proximity to don't like her choices for herself.

This woman talks like she is a church attender (at least on feast days or whatever they called days like Christmas and

Easter in those days), one well versed in the legend of God, but not acquainted with the person of God. Listen to her quote the concepts with confidence. She has all the Sunday School answers.

Read on and get the rest of the story. When she realizes that the man she is talking with has firsthand knowledge of the Creator who can put her life together in the masterpiece He created just for her, her life changes. With Christ involved in her life picture, she becomes the evangelist to the entire community and the community responds to this broken and now reconstructed (at least partially) masterpiece in such an awesome way that Christ later sees the results of her message to the community and says, "The fields are white to harvest." The white is the robes of all the people coming to see this puzzle rebuilder and masterpiece remaker.

Another story is of a woman caught in the very act of adultery. It is found in John 8:2-11;

2 And early in the morning he came again into the temple, and all the people came unto him; and he sat down, and taught them.

3 And the scribes and Pharisees brought unto him a woman taken in adultery; and when they had set her in the midst,

4 They say unto him, Master, this woman was taken in adultery, in the very act.

5 Now Moses in the law commanded us, that such should be stoned: but what sayest thou?

6 This they said, tempting him, that they might have to accuse him. But Jesus stooped down, and with his finger wrote on the ground, as though he heard them not.

7 So when they continued asking him, he lifted up himself, and said unto them, He that is without sin among you, let him first cast a stone at her.

8 And again he stooped down, and wrote on the ground.

9 And they which heard it, being convicted by their own conscience, went out one by one, beginning at the eldest, even unto the last: and Jesus was left alone, and the woman standing in the midst.

10 When Jesus had lifted up himself, and saw none but the woman, he said unto her, Woman, where are those thine accusers? hath no man condemned thee?

11 She said, No man, Lord. And Jesus said unto her, Neither do I condemn thee: go, and sin no more. KJV

Here is another woman who has been putting herself together through the pleasures of this world. Pleasures are not very good glue. They tend to fall apart at the first sign of trouble. That glue is tear soluble, and there are many tears in the pleasures of this world.

Where is the other half of the sin in this story? Why is the man not present? My Mama used to say, "What's good for the goose is good for the gander." Why wasn't the man dragged to the feet of Jesus also? Could he have been too strong for some of the old geezer Pharisees and fought his way to freedom? Was he the one setting up the young lady to begin with? There are a multitude of questions without answers in this story.

It is very difficult to put something together out of questions without knowing the answers. We can see that Jesus offered to her a way to the real masterpiece of her life rather than the pathway she had been following up to the point where her self-construed puzzle fell apart.

Then there is the story of David in 2 Samuel 11

1 And it came to pass, after the year was expired, at the time when kings go forth to battle, that David sent Joab, and his servants with him, and all Israel; and they destroyed the children of Ammon, and besieged Rabbah. But David tarried still at Jerusalem.

2 And it came to pass in an eveningtide, that David arose from off his bed, and walked upon the roof of the king's house: and from the roof he saw a woman washing herself; and the woman was very beautiful to look upon.

3 And David sent and inquired after the woman. And one said, Is not this Bath-sheba, the daughter of Eliam, the wife of Uriah the Hittite?

4 And David sent messengers, and took her; and she came in unto him, and he lay with her; for she was purified from her uncleanness: and she returned unto her house.

5 And the woman conceived, and sent and told David, and said, I am with child. KJV

David has it all. Every piece is nicely fitted together even after all the trials with King Saul and then with his first wife. It must have been a truly beautiful masterpiece hanging at the peak of Jerusalem only one step from the place God's Temple would reside.

David looked to enhance his puzzle with a new section. He looked on Bath-sheba with lust, committed adultery, set her husband up to die, and took her to wife. He was living high until a fella sent from God makes him face the music and then the baby dies. (2 Samuel 11) God ripped that section apart because it wasn't supposed to be there. God had never painted that episode in the masterpiece called David. God then drew in some new parts as consequences of the errors in David's life. None of us would like those next episodes of David's life puzzle. Incestuously raped daughter, dead sons, battle against a son who takes the throne and sleeps publicly with David's concubines; and then blood, blood, and more blood, with a topper of not being able to build the Temple of God just don't seem like fun things to have included in my puzzle. How about you?

In each case, and we could look at many more, including my own life or yours, without God the Creator and Masterpiece Painter involved in the process of putting us together after we have scattered our pieces all over the place a mess was created. We have pieces everywhere. Some are in storage vaults. Others are in our pockets. Many of our pieces we don't have or even suspect they even exist. Most of the pieces we have in our possession are not even pieces to our puzzle. So, how do we complete our puzzle from this point? Let's see if we can figure it out.

"Neither is there salvation in any other: for there is none other name under heaven given among men, whereby we must be saved." (Acts 4:12)

The words "salvation" and "saved" are used here. Salvation as translated here means to be safe from some life threatening or really tough situation. In this case, it refers to being safe from the consequences of trying to put our own puzzle together after we have sinned and scattered the pieces hither and yon.

The "saved" is the word we want to look at in this passage. Here it refers to "salvation" but it also carries with it the idea of "made complete." Okay, follow along here. In the King James translation the idea of complete is expressed in the word "Perfect." To be made perfect is to be made complete. Let's look at a couple of passages.

There was a man in the land of Uz, whose name was Job; and that man was perfect and upright, and one that feared God, and eschewed evil. (Job 1:1)

Be ye therefore perfect, even as your Father which is in heaven is perfect. (Matthew 5:48)

Are ye so foolish? having begun in the Spirit, are ye now made perfect by the flesh? (Galatians 3:3)

Night and day praying exceedingly that we might see your face, and might perfect that which is lacking in your faith. (1 Thessalonians 3:10)

Each of these has the word "perfect" where a better choice of words is "complete."

We are looking to become complete. We desire ourselves

to be put together just the way the Master Artist has set before us. We don't want incompleteness or a shoddy picture or an ugly thing, we want the beauty that was designed for us from before the foundations of creation were set in place.

In each of the above references we see that there is a connection between completeness and God. Either God is connected to the idea of being complete or someone teaching us of God is in His place. Without any effort at all we come to the realization that without God we are not going to become complete, our masterpiece will never be put together properly, and we will never be all our Creator wanted us to be.

Let's look at the masterpiece for a moment here. When we go to the art museum and look at the paintings or whatever is presented there, we find ourselves saying, "Oh, isn't this artist great!" or "Wow, that artist has no concept of beauty, that piece is ugly."

I can remember a time when I thought that I could be artistic. After all, my mother was, my father was, many members of the previous generation were, why not give it a whirl?

Ugh, that piece is ugly. I am not an artist in the masterpiece sense. I am not an artist in any sense. No one would ever look at anything I have done and give it high praise, unless it was the critic who declared the paintings done by the elephant at the Phoenix Zoo to be great art.

The work of real art brings praise to the artist. When we are put together properly it brings praise and honor to the artist. When our lives reflect the masterpiece from the Creator's living room, He alone deserves the praise, honor and glory.

Let's think about Solomon for a moment. God offered to build him a tremendous masterpiece. God gave Solomon riches beyond his wildest dreams and imaginings. God then asked him what he really wanted. Solomon only wanted to be a better king of God's people so he asked for wisdom to rule well.

That's a pretty good start, don't you think.

Now look at the rest of the story. As the rest of Solomon's life moves along, his many wives and concubines (about a thousand or so) begin to put his pieces together rather than Solomon allowing God to continue the job He started. The result is the book of Ecclesiastes where Solomon describes the emptiness of a life lived that doesn't follow the plan God had painted before the beginning. His summation of that life is "Vanity of vanities; all is vanity;" vanity being defined as emptiness or like a wisp of smoke.

Isn't that a sad commentary on a life? He had it all and all was empty, nothing of any substance, just a wisp of smoke.

Okay, enough preaching, the question is how do we find the Creator in order to get Him to put us together properly?

"Oh! Oh! I know teacher, I know, I know," cries little Suzy from the front row.

"How do we do that, Suzy?"

"We go to church, teacher."

We go looking for a church to find God in so He can put us together.

Chapter 8

THE CHURCH MYTH

Most of us have tried church on various occasions, most of those times associated with weddings, funerals, or as a kid because our parents dragged us there or even during periods of trial in our lives. (That was my drug problem, they drug me to church 2 or 3 or even 4 times a week.) Some of us found the experience somewhat lacking in comfort or in bringing about change in our lives. We find ourselves shook up by the fire and brimstone shouting or we can't stand the dirges sung by a choir and/or congregation with totally empty or, even worse, sad expressions on their faces.

We want to be happy and know the joy of having it together, not the drudgery of gotta-do's and if-you-don'ts. We want to be something, but definitely not that. We want to have something, but definitely not what they are selling. Join? NO WAY!

One of the reasons that church cannot help you is a church is just a building. Buildings do not build. People build. People build churches, not vice versa. Just as we build our custom personal gods, churches reflect the folks that build them. When man builds a church it goes nowhere and does nothing, when God builds a Church watch out, anything can and will happen to His glory and honor. Man built churches can become unhealthy addictions in themselves. But, we will get to that later. Hang in there.

Deep in each person's masterpiece is a puzzle piece shaped like the Church. (What could be the difference between church and Church? Think about it for later.) It is a foundation piece. It is faintly colored and deftly camouflaged by the Master Painter. It is really hard to find. It must be, so many people spend most of their lives looking for the one church that will meet all their needs and put them together into the wonderful person that they want to be. Not many pay much attention to the church teacher that challenges them to be what the Creator wants them to be.

We not only have designer gods floating around out there, we have designer churches. Designer churches promise life in abundance, not God's abundance, but blab it and grab it theology, you can be all you want to be, and the last-but-not-least promise, if you have enough faith your wildest dreams will materialize and you will be eternally happy.

Grandma used to call that hogwash. Mom called it boloney. The cowboy next door called it . . . Never mind.

Church cannot do a thing for you.

Your friends cannot do a thing for you.

No one can do a thing for you.

Some can enable you, but cannot do a thing for you.

Enabling can be good or bad.

At this point you are really getting frustrated with this aren't you?

Have you ever read "The Velveteen Rabbit"? In that children's book (I really think it was written for adults), horse explains to the Velveteen Rabbit how one becomes real. That's what we're after here isn't it? We want to be the real thing that the Creator wanted us to be from the beginning. The bottom line horse told the rabbit is that he must submit to be a servant for the kids. It is the kids that chose the rabbit and only the kids can make him real.

It is God who designed us and only God can make us real. Here we realize that we must submit to God and allow

Him to put us together. It isn't the church. It isn't friends. It is God. Hey, we've been here before, last chapter, as a matter of fact. But, now there is a new dimension. Submit. That was a key in horse's statement to the rabbit. Did you catch it?

Submit.

All of us start out as one-of-a-kind originals, but in going our own way with our own designer god and in our own designer church we become just like everybody else. In submission to the Creator, we find the only way to be the unique, original, one-of-a-kind servant of God He created us to be.

Think about it. Think on how hard we struggle to be our own person only to become just like everyone else. That is not what God intended for us to be. We are each to become a self for Him, not a crowd for self.

We can now go to any church that teaches the Creator God of the Bible and find what we need to put us together. We can go in a closet and find Him also. How about on a stroll thru the park? You can find God anywhere in His creation, and that is everywhere.

Go ahead, submit.

"How do I do that?" you ask.

You say, "Okay, God, I am yours. Put me together the way You had intended me to be put together from the Beginning." Say it in all faith, belief, trust, sincerity, and commitment, and then let Him do it His way.

Sounds easy, doesn't it?

It is and then again, it isn't.

God's Word, the Bible, says that no man or woman can come directly to God except through Jesus Christ. (John 14:6) We cannot submit directly because we are sinners. Because we are sinners it takes a sacrifice to atone for that sin. (Hebrews 9:22)

It takes a sacrifice that is perfect in every way. Because we are sinners, we are imperfect. Since we are imperfect, we cannot die to pay the price for our own sins. Christ was perfect. He never sinned. Therefore, Christ was that sacrifice for us and that is what we must have faith in – that Christ, who knew no sin (2 Corinthians 5:21), could be the perfect sacrifice on the Cross of Calvary for our sins and through faith in that Christ we can have access to God. (Hebrews 10:20)

The Bible says that we submit to God through faith in Jesus Christ. (John 3:16) When we have faith in Jesus Christ, He asks God the Father to send His Holy Spirit to live within us as the seal on our lives that we have submitted to Him. (Ephesians 1:13-14, 4:30) Not only the official seal of God on our lives, but a down payment for all the promises He has in store for us. Then and only then can we become the real masterpiece of God.

Now we run into a real problem. We find out very quickly that God does not put us together. You saw that coming, didn't you? Jesus doesn't put us together. The church doesn't either. Not even the friends and loved ones we have.

Don't give up!

The good news is that the Holy Spirit within us gives us the power to put ourselves together the way God had intended for us to be put together to begin with.

There are some who might argue with that statement and use references to "new creation" (2 Corinthians 5:17) and "renewing your mind" (Romans 12:1) or "the mind of Christ," (Philippians 2:5) but the statement is true and so are their points of argument. Just check out folks from the Bible that God has worked with like Benaiah, Jabez, Peter, and others, God really put them together as unique individuals.

We are at the moment of sincere faith that Jesus Christ died to pay the penalty for our sins, a new creation. The old picture that we have been messing around with in our own way is gone and the real one is growing in its place. Our mind is renewed. It is renewed to think like Christ and to act like Christ because our picture is coming together in His image. (Remember, all the masterpieces were painted in the image of

God which is God the Son.)

Remember how we said that church cannot help you? Well, Church can. Church, with a capital C, is the body of believers on earth, living for Him as He died for them. The Biblical term, Body of Christ, is that collection of believers and is living eternally already.

While God has given us the power though His Holy Spirit, we must do the work, we must become the complete picture by using the renewed mind and the ideas it presents. I am referring to the ideas of running from evil and pursuing righteousness, (1 Peter 3:11) putting on the armor of God, (Ephesians 6) keeping ourselves from sin (1 Peter 3:11) loving one another, (John 15:12) being transformed by the renewing of our minds, (Romans 12:1-2) and so many others. *We* are told to do those things.

God does not take away our freedom in submission; He grants us total freedom, real freedom with power beyond our wildest dreams. We can do all things because of Him. (Philippians 4:13) All the things we need to do, He gives us the power to do. That power is the Holy Spirit. (Acts 18) The new us allows us to be the masterpieces that cause others to give God the praise for empowering such an awesome picture that others can see. (Matthew 5:16

Chapter 9

THE FIRST PIECES THAT MATTER

Let's take a look at the masterpiece that is _____ (put in your name) at this point.

Since you have followed along this far and if you have truly taken each of the previous chapters to heart, putting your faith in Jesus because you want to be all God wanted you to be in the Beginning, you will have the following pieces available to you and in place.

Just as three colors are blended to make all colors, three persons of the Three-in-One Godhead will now blend together to make you all that you can be.

Dead center in all that is you is the God the Father piece. It is spirit. The Bible tells us that God is spirit and must be worshiped in spirit. You might picture this piece as the canvas of the masterpiece that is you. It undergirds everything that is you. It is your foundation. Hang onto it for dear life.

The second piece and the only one visible, so far, is the God the Son, Jesus, piece. It is shaped like an empty tomb with the faint impression of a cross before it; because Jesus, who knew no sin, became sin for you and died on the cross in your place. His entire purpose was completed on the cross. He then rose from the dead out of a borrowed tomb to show us there is a way out of spiritual death (due to sin) to life, to *real* life in God. So, the cross is very important, but the empty tomb indicates the completion of all God's work to bring us real spiritual life, life eternal. The empty tomb entrance reminds us that we may only get to God through Jesus Christ. As He went through death into life, we must also go through Him to get to God and in Jesus Christ is life. The Bible tells us that by Him, Jesus, were all things made and by Him all things are held together. Therefore, without Him there is no rightful construction and all attempts to get it together without him just fall apart.

The third piece we have at this point is the God the Holy Spirit piece. It, too, is Spirit and therefore also invisible. The Holy Spirit piece is God the Father's gift to us at the request of God the Son, Jesus. (John 14-17) This piece aligns the pieces of the Masterpiece that is you together and holds them in proper position. We are told that at this point we are sealed (glued together and imprinted) by the Holy Spirit until God fulfills all His promises in our lives. Think of the Holy Spirit as permanent Super Metamorphic Puzzle Piece Aligner and Supernatural Stickum. It also gives us the power to know the pieces that are really us and put those pieces that are really us in their proper place at the correct time.

Because our puzzle is or will be made up of many pieces, it is very fragile. Think about it. You are working on a puzzle on the dining room table. Your baby brother, little brat that he is, walks into the room and climbs up on a chair across the table from you to see what you are doing. He watches for a moment or two before saying, "Whatcha doin'?" You carefully explain puzzles to your darling little brother, showing him the box top picture and place a piece into its proper position in the half finished masterpiece before you. What does little brother, sweet baby brother, do? He grabs the nearest piece, climbs onto the table and proceeds to cram, rip, snap, knot, fold, spindle and mutilate your hours of hard labor trying, honestly trying as only a fantastic baby brother can be, to make that piece fit into the puzzle. That's the reason we need the Super Metaphoric Puzzle Piece Aligner, and Supernatural Stickum. Even the Devil himself cannot break the hold the Holy Spirit has on us as God's masterpiece.

And, don't forget all those pieces you have been grabbing up and hoarding all over the place. You have them, but are they the real you? Many of them will not be yours, but how do you tell. If they are not the real you, you probably won't much like the person they make you or what they do for you. You may even sense that there are major pieces missing or at least misplaced. You don't like who you are because they make you someone you were not designed to be by the Master Painter of the Universe.

Now is the time to become the person that is really you.

Are you ready?

Picture a real jigsaw puzzle. Matter of fact, go into the closet and get a puzzle, a kids puzzle with big pieces would be a big help. Find two pieces that fit together. Put them together. Take them apart. Put them together.

What do you notice about these pieces?

Do they fit together easily?

Do they bring the whole picture a little closer to completion?

Do you feel a sense of accomplishment when you have them together?

I'll wager that the pieces have notches and bulges that just slide together with only the slightest hint of effort and that you are very satisfied, a sense of completing something, when you find two pieces that fit together.

Now, remember that one piece you have been left with and carry around with you everywhere trying to find another piece to join it to? Try fitting it with the Jesus piece. Fits, doesn't it?

We find that we have a real powerful joining relationship with Jesus which ties us to the Jesus piece on the Father piece thru the power of the Super Metamorphic Puzzle Piece Aligner Holy Spirit piece. Jesus prays to the Father in John 17 that those He died for would become one with Him just as He is one with the Father and the Holy Spirit. Through a personal relationship with Jesus we become one with the other three pieces already in place.

Once we truly submit to God thru a faith relationship with Christ, Grace kicks in and our spirit (that one piece we have held onto all these years) is joined to the Jesus piece by the Holy Spirit of God and we become one spirit.(1 Corinthians 6:17,19) Because we are one Spirit we now have the Holy Spirit guiding us in the task of putting us together. We look in the mirror we see the glory (attributes) of the Lord (2 Corinthians 3:18) because the Spirit of the Lord allows us to see them. When we remove the blindfold from our eyes thru the power of the Holy Spirit, we see ourselves as we can be, as we are supposed to be, and not as we have been seeing ourselves. There is now a sense of completeness, a feeling of filling the hole in our lives, just like when we place the last piece in an earthly puzzle on the kitchen table.

We now have a goal in life that has eternal purpose. That goal is to become like the image the Spirit shows us in that mirror. We have the attributes and it is now up to us to make it happen.

INTERLUDE

The puzzle has begun God's way. Up to this point most of what has happened has happened in a moment of belief beyond description. All that follows may appear to be sequential, but in reality are more probably random events in the completion of the masterpiece that is you.

Chapter 10

NO LIMITS AND A RABBIT TRAIL

We find out the most amazing thing at this time. We find that our masterpiece is an unlimited masterpiece. There are no edge pieces. Our masterpiece has no limits, no boundaries, because God has no limits and God is our canvas. The only limitation is us. We are the limiting factor.

What we find in all these individuals through whom God has written Biblical history is that faith gives you the confidence to adapt to your circumstances while never compromising your convictions.

You either adapt when you face circumstances you cannot control, or you allow them to become boundaries of your life that will establish the parameters of your freedom, define your limits and diminish your dreams – and that is where you stop. (McManus, Erwin Raphael, Wide Awake, Thomas Nelson, 2008, p72)

You have been painted to be a flexible, growing, thinking, multi-purpose being that God has put in place to carry on His works.(Ephesians 2:10)

Think about it, *you* are the only thing holding you back at this point. 2 Corinthians 3:17 says we have liberty. We now have the permission, power, and passion to become like the image in the mirror. That image is the image of the living Lord, Jesus Christ. This is why folks say things like, "I am becoming more like Christ every day," or as Paul said, "I am keeping my eye on the goal, the goal of being like Christ."(Philippians 3:14, 2 Timothy 4:6-7)

Let's take a rabbit trail!

Liberty is an interesting word to look at. Liberty means you can do exactly what you want to. It is freedom, liberation, authorization and independence all rolled into one word. God says you have "perfect liberty" as a person submitted to Him.

How can we be God's person, submitted to Him, and still do anything we want with this perfect liberty?

I am truly glad that you asked that question.

God gives us liberty, complete liberty, perfect liberty. We CAN do anything we want to do. Yes, you can stay out as late as you want to, eat all the ice cream you desire, and even do horrendous things like David (you know, murder and adultery just to name a couple). Remember when I introduced liberty in this passage? I said we now have the permission, power and passion to become like the image in the mirror. Does the image in the mirror stay out as late as he wants, eat all the ice cream he desires, or commit adultery and murder?

NO! Liberty without responsibility is license. God does not give license.

Now that we have perfect liberty we are guided by God's promise in Psalm 37:4, *"Delight thyself in the Lord; and he shall give thee the desires of thine heart."* (KJV) To use my liberty to translate this a bit, it says, "When you find your joy and happiness in Christ, He will then give you all you want in your heart." Hang with me for a minute. This isn't blab it and grab it theology, this is God's Word. There is something here that is so subtle that it rivals the faint church at the bottom of the masterpiece that is you.

When you are submitted totally to God, your wants, your desires become completely different from the desires you had the moment before you submitted. Before it was things, now it is a concept that is wrapped up in Christ, in the Kingdom of God, in living for Jesus as He died for you. A new car or bigger house doesn't matter anymore, what matters is the furthering of the Kingdom of God. Because that is what matters now, two things change in our lives.

The first is that we want to please God. Instead of pleasing ourselves or other folks, we become God pleasers. We no longer want to please man except in the circumstances where it is a part of pleasing God. We want this so much that we no longer think about who we are pleasing, instead we supernaturally carry out this task without conscious effort. After all, are we not guided and aligned by the Holy Spirit of God? Since we submit to Him to lead, every step we take is in His direction, God pleasing.

The second change is that things are not important except those things necessary to carry out God's directions in our life.

Thinking on both of these I find that the two changes are really one. Let's sum it up with a colloquial statement, "We don't gotta do anything, our joy is to wanna do what God wants us to do and then do it." Bottom line, plain and simple. (1 Corinthians 10:23) This all comes about through submission. We receive from that submission the permission, power, and passion to be all that God desired for us to be from before the beginning of time. Jesus said many times, "If you love me, keep my commandments. (John 14:15 and many others)" That is a command and a test. The sign of our real faith in Jesus is keeping the commandments because we wanna.

We CAN do anything we want to within our physical power; spiritually our delight is in the Word of God, His commands. Therefore, we do not want to do those things that are not in His will, those things that are sin, those things that discredit all He has done for us. We want to share the joy of the Lord, not the pain of sin, with a world that is watching God working in us to piece by piece shape us into the masterpiece He painted.

We have submitted.

Back to no limits.

We have realized that our masterpiece is one with no limits, no edge pieces. Yeah, there are guidelines we might call boundaries, boundaries that keep us out of the swamps and muck of sin, the entanglements of poisonous weeds in our masterpiece, and boundaries that guide us in His directions. All of these are great boundaries that we can step over at any time, but don't want to because to do so would separate us from Him.

Since our puzzle has no edge pieces, not limits as we generally think of limits, we realize we are building from some point outward. This is definitely not the way most folks put together a puzzle. There may be others but the closest to a boundary-less puzzle is a 3-D one I saw in a high dollar novelty (as in rich folks toys) shop of a globe of planet earth. The complete puzzle was a hollow sphere covered with a satellite photo montage of the features in 3-D on the surface. I would surmise you would just start with just any piece and begin building that puzzle. Even it had severe, strict limits, but no edges. Once all the pieces were properly in place there was nowhere else to go and nothing else to do with it but look at it or put it back in the box.

Our masterpiece puzzle has no such restrictions that are discernible to us. Only God knows the final size, shape, and extent of us.

Now, find a human created puzzle, open the box, pull out one random piece, and place it in the middle of the dining room table. Lonely looking thing isn't it? Beginning from that piece, build the rest of the puzzle. Oh, yeah, you cannot look at the box top picture for assistance. Just randomly pull out one piece at a time and try to fit it, and then, if it doesn't fit put it back in the box.

Is it any wonder we need Divine intervention to build our life properly?

It is a tough, exhausting task, this puzzle of ours, and we

are moving and building it through and in God's direction. Ken Hemphill said in his book, *EKG*, "You never get the feeling you have seen all this before." We have sensed this new direction and liberty in our life. For the first time in our life we are focused on moving ahead with a heart for tomorrow like never before. An excited exhaustion leads to a good night's sleep.

Chapter 11

SOMETHING IS MISSING

When you awaken in the morning the first thing you do is rush to the mirror and check the masterpiece that is you. The God piece is there undergirding all that is you providing support and a platform to build upon. The Spirit piece is there ready to guide you to all that God has created in and for you. The Jesus piece with its empty tomb is there as the anchor piece for all else to connect to. As you begin to turn away you are stopped dead in your tracks with the realization that there is something missing.

You examine the masterpiece of God even more closely checking out all there is until the realization that it is not a piece that is missing, but an image in the Jesus piece. The empty tomb opening no longer has the faint impression of a cross before it. Now, where did that go?

Jesus said to his disciples as recorded in Luke 9:23,"*If any man will come after me, let him deny himself, and take up his cross daily, and follow me.*" Here we are in a new day with a cross missing. The reason is that we must take up our cross daily according to Jesus. We have committed ourselves to be followers (imitators) of Jesus Christ, slept on that idea with great excitement and awakened to find the cross missing in the puzzle of our life.

We have not taken it up for this day.

What does it mean to take up a cross?

Wow! You ask the greatest questions.

Since we are now followers of Christ we must look to Him for the example in order to answer this question. Philippians 2:5-8 gives us the answer with, *"Your attitude should be the kind that was shown us by Jesus Christ, who, though he was God, did not demand and cling to his rights as God, but laid aside his mighty power and glory, taking the disguise of a slave and becoming like men. And he humbled himself even further, going so far as actually to die a criminal's death on a cross.* (TLB)

To take up a cross is to die.

If you read on in Philippians 2 you will find that Jesus died for the service of others. He lived for service and died that you and I might live. He died to pay the price for our sins so that we might one day enter the presence of God through the simplicity of faith. He died a criminal's death even though He had never done anything wrong. Before He died He lived a life that exemplified the perfect masterpiece. He lived in service to others. Christ showed us how to love, to really love, in spite of the responses received from others.

In order to do that Jesus put aside all the glory that was His as God. Think on that for just a bit. What is it like to live in Heaven? Total perfection coupled with complete power in the ultimate beauty would be one way of labeling Heaven. Christ gave all that up to become a man, a man servant, in order to totally serve all mankind. And now He says if we would follow Him, we must do the same thing.

Did you look at the words "deny himself" in this Luke reference? The Philippians 2 passage shows us the meaning for Him and for us. He denied all that He had, all that He was, and all that He wanted in order to accomplish all that needed to be done for the glory of God. We are to do the same thing.

We are to reject all our wants, rights, and desires in order to do all God has designed for us to accomplish in the masterpiece that He painted so long ago. Like a criminal we give up all to be incarcerated in Christ. Oh, what a velvet prison with total freedom!

As He died for us, He asks us to live for Him and

sometimes even to die a martyr's death for the cause of the Kingdom of God. No, He won't ask you to strap explosives around your middle and blow yourself up in a crowded marketplace. Yes, He does ask us to love others enough to share the message, to be a witness to the truth that led you to be a follower of Christ even if it leads to death because of your message. The very word "witness" comes from the same root word as "martyr" in the Greek of the New Testament.

This whole idea of denying ourselves and taking up our cross is summed up in Galatians 2:20 when Paul writes of himself at the leading of the Holy Spirit, *"I am crucified with Christ: nevertheless I live; yet not I, but Christ lives in me: and the life which I now live in the flesh I live by the faith of the Son of God, who loved me, and gave himself for me."* He says he, Paul, has died to self with Christ and lives for Christ, through faith in Christ, who loved him enough to die for him.

Every day when your eyes open you give that day up to service for the glory of God, the benefit of the Kingdom of God, and the cross faintly depicted before the tomb on the Jesus piece becomes your cross for another day of following Christ. To begin with this must be a conscious effort, which, as the days of our lives in Him go by, will become more and more of an unconscious habit as we rise every morning to focus our lives on His will, not our will. Then, and only then, the core of the masterpiece will be made complete for the beginning of each day as we look in the mirror. Only God knows what it will look like as we accumulate more pieces throughout that day in service to Him.

So, we pray hard first and proceed boldly. If we don't pray we will not proceed, no matter what we try.

Chapter 12

CALLED TO OUR PIECES

Three or four pieces aren't much of a masterpiece. The Bible does tell us that we are made complete in Jesus Christ. (2 Corinthians 2:10) Four pieces bring us into the presence of God. If we were to die at this moment in our lives, we would enter into our final reward with God. The vast majority of us will live longer than this moment and there must be a reason for our continuing to live. "What is that reason?" and "Why am I here?" are driving questions of mankind. We must move on in Christ in order to answer those questions by completing the puzzle.

Somehow we must acquire the rest of the pieces to the puzzle that is us. Nothing in God's creation is simple. There must be more to us than four pieces, particularly when three of those pieces have existed forever; God, the Father, the Son, and the Holy Spirit. We do know that there are many pieces floating around. We have a hoard of them stashed in many different closets and storage spaces, many of which we may have even forgotten. Most likely, we are still collecting, trying to find ourselves and all that entails.

At this point we would wander around lost except for the Holy Spirit who has connected our spirit with the Spirit of God to make a communication link, an out of this world wireless service (you know, like an megaG network that is free) with a direct connection to God that is telling us there are more pieces of our masterpiece and pointing us in the direction of those pieces.

The Bible tells us to never be under the control of anything except the Holy Spirit of God.(Ephesians 5:18) Being the good little masterpieces that we are, we allow ourselves to be controlled by the Holy Spirit to the point of being guided to the next piece. In the churchy world, this being led is labeled a 'call' from God. We have already answered the first call from God. We have been led by the teaching of the Word and conviction of the Holy Spirit to God. That is His call for us to come to Him. Jesus is quoted as saying that when He is on the cross He will call all mankind to Himself (John 12:22) and the only way to the Father is through Himself (John 14:6). We have all received this call. Some folks have responded to God's call to Himself through the Son. That call got our one piece to join in relationship with the important first three pieces of our masterpiece.

Now we are being called to service. All who are called to God are called to service. Service is being God's servant to this world He has created. We can picture each call to service as a call to a cache of pieces or maybe just one piece. This call is specific to each individual and must be searched out. Prayer plays a big part in this, then just going where God guides you will get you where you are supposed to be.

While all the pieces may appear to be the same value to our human eyes, some of the pieces we are led to are spiritually large and cover a lot of the canvas of our lives. These are the big calls that have a great impact for God and His Kingdom. Many of the calls we receive are just little incidental things. Actual spiritual value will depend on the eternal impact of the call which we may never know until we are in His presence.

You might be called to attend a university and get an education in an area God is preparing to use you. This would certainly be a fairly high valued piece in our mind because it becomes a major part of who you are. Then there is the call to the small things in life, like helping a person cross the street or simply saying a nice word to someone. Not much impact there, you probably won't even remember it, small value for you, but large for Him, maybe. Think of all the stories where a simple act changed the life of an individual, a person who has gone on to impact even more that the person doing the simple act.

You may have saved a life with the nice word. Then again, you might have gained nothing more than a foothold on your call through all of the education you have received.

Each piece is acquired by the simplicity of obedience to the leading of the Holy Spirit. Only God knows the value or cost of each piece in the eternal scheme of things.

Ephesians 2:10 tells us that you are called to good works lined up just for you from before the creation. Now you are finding them and each is a piece of you in Christ.

Some pieces are easy to acquire. Perhaps it is easy for you to study the Bible for 30 minutes each day or to serve close to home at the soup kitchen just down the road. These are easy pieces, but valued, important pieces nonetheless. Some of us will be called to leave easy behind and go to tough places where the pieces are difficult to find and even harder to grasp, such as being a worker in a foreign country, or working in the inner city, or maybe in a barren desert filled with heat, poisonous snakes, and other life threatening dangers. The high value important pieces will always require us to leave our comfort zone and enter the unknown for unexplained reasons. Some of us don't seem to have a call at all as they continue where they are, doing what they have been doing; God is using us here in ways that are difficult or sometimes impossible to know. Through all of this, the opposition (the devil and his troops) will try to lead us astray with false calls, stinking thinking of our minds or roaming eyes, and just plain pride in ourselves and our stuff.

Our stuff is all we think we possess. I have heard too many times people saying, "I am sensing a call to do, go, be
_____, but I just can't leave my _____ behind." God has given us all we have just as He has given us all we are and can be. Our stuff is to be used for God's Glory. Sometimes it will be used for our own benefit and other times for the benefit of others. Stuff is always the wrong anchor in the storm of life. Have you ever wondered how much stuff goes from yard sale to thrift shop to yard sale to white elephant gift ad nauseum, without ever being really used other than as a paper weight in the garage or storeroom?

I know a couple, Norm and Teri, who heard God's call to Taiwan. They immediately sold or gave away everything including their old dog, thereby reducing their stuff to four suitcases and went. That is the way to answer the Call of God!

Many times the service God wants of us in that place, that time, with those people or even one person is to tell what God has done in your life. We call that witnessing or testifying. What do those two words say to you? I picture a person on a chair to the right of a judge in a large room telling what they know about something being considered in that room, only the facts and always the truth. You got it? A courtroom where a witness or expert in a trial telling what they know, saw, heard, felt, or said in a particular set of circumstances. No opinions unless asked, only the facts as they occurred or known concerning whatever is on trial.

God is always on trial.

We are His expert witnesses.

That isn't really hard for you to do. You lived it, you tell it. What has God done for, to, in, and through you? You are the only expert on you, other than God.

If the call is so important, how can we tell it is the call of God and not a call from the dark side (evil)?

That is another great question and I am really glad you asked it.

One thing we do know for sure, the call of God in your life will be righteous, in other words in accordance with God's Word. He will never call you to murder someone, lie, cheat, steal, deal unfairly with, or otherwise go against His own attributes and in accordance with Scriptural guidance. If we had the time to look at all the calls recorded in Scripture we would find four common factors within them all.

1. Each person called knew it was God.

2. Each understood exactly what was being said.

3. Each understood the action that would be required to carry out the call.

4. Each went through a crisis of faith (do it or don't).

To sum it up in the words of Oswald Chambers in his great daily devotional My Utmost for His Highest, "*The call is the expression of the nature from which it comes, and we can only record the call if the same nature is in us.*" In other words, when the call is from God and you have the Holy Spirit dwelling within you, you will know it is the call for you from God.

Chapter 13

A TIME FOR CLEANING

Remember all those pieces you have been storing up? A few of them might be yours. An enormous number of them will belong to other folks' puzzles. And then, taking that same thought next door to your neighbors' house, your neighbors all have a collection of pieces. Some of their pieces will belong in your puzzle. To complicate the problem even more folks all over the world may have pieces of you and many others, just as you have theirs.

Since we are led by the Holy Spirit as sealed servants of our Creator, we are led to our pieces no matter where they are and we are led to others to deliver pieces to them so that they can be completed just as we are being completed. Does that make sense? God knows the whole BIG PICTURE and even knows where all the pieces are at any given point in time. He will lead us to complete His picture of us as long as we are willing to be led.

Some people will be led to others to share the story of how they began to get it all together so more folks can begin to get themselves put together. We have called that testifying or witnessing. We share the story of God's love toward us with others so that they can know God's love towards them and begin the process of putting it all together for God's Glory.

There are occasions where we will just be called upon to give pieces and receive nothing in return. These meetings could be called "missions" to people who have never heard the Good News of the Masterpiece Painter and His awesome picture of them. Who knows, maybe someday when they understand better, they will discover pieces in their possession that are ours and return the favor by delivering pieces to us in return. Or, God may just deliver pieces to us as a blessing for our faithful service of going, giving and testifying expecting nothing in return.

Other meetings will occur where we only receive. These are those chance meetings where we bless someone else by being the receiver for whatever reason, allowing them to serve us and thereby they obtain the blessing from God. When we allow someone to bless or serve us even when we don't really need it is an example of this. You know, all those neighborhood plates of cookies at Christmas time and such.

A large number of relationships will occur where we will give and receive.

As we go thru life led by the Holy Spirit each person and situation will reveal more and more pieces to the big picture that is us. Sometimes major portions of the puzzle will just fall into place, while at other times in our lives it seems as if every person and every situation is a barren desert with nothing to add to the masterpiece that is us. These deserts are a time to reflect, a time to take inventory, and a time to consolidate.

Every desert is marked by the sense of going nowhere, accomplishing nothing and/or taken-for-granted relationships. It is in these apparently empty places we can truly reflect on what has been put together, how far we have come and where we sense God leading us. We can use the quiet and stability of this time to examine the roads we have traveled in search of ourselves. The best part of these desert times is the monastic atmosphere of spiritual retreat allowing us to examine our relationship with God thru Jesus Christ and then our relationships with others. We need these from time to time.

The desert time allows us to check the alignment of every

piece and look for missing pieces and gaps, ensuring that all pieces are God given and held together by His Holy Spirit and not plugged in to a place of our choosing and not a part of God's design for us.

I find that I need a day or two a month to spend just examining myself, my relationships and the total puzzle that is me on His canvas getting all the pieces properly aligned in their proper places. Many times I find myself just sitting or wandering around doing not much of anything except listening and filing pieces in their appropriate spots. The quieter and fewer distractions the better it is for me. I am easily distracted by the glory of God's creation around me which allows me a greater opportunity to refocus my entire being on the Creator. When my Creator guided tour of me is over I am in a much better condition mentally and physically. My wife even tells me I am easier to live with after realignment like this.

Of course we still have the choice of going His way or not. We can refuse to share pieces. We can say, "No" to the missions God calls us to, the relief of the poor and the downtrodden. We can even ignore the widows. The orphans and the hungry are not a problem if we don't hear their cries or otherwise deny their existence. We can even allow the government to take care of them, if we so choose. Don't you wonder what will be missing in your puzzle if you leave those things out? I do. If you are choosing not to do according to God's leading, you must use this time to evaluate your relationship with God thru Jesus Christ. Is He really the canvas of your world? Or more bluntly, are you truly His child?

1 John 2:3-6 in the NCV says,

"We can be sure that we know God if we obey his commands. Anyone who says, 'I know God,' but does not obey God's commands is a liar, and the truth is not in that person. But if someone obeys God's teaching, then in that person God's love has truly reached it

goal. This is how we can be sure we are living in God: Whoever says that he lives in God must live as Jesus lived."

Reflect on this passage. Then go back and read the paragraph before the Bible quote. If you are choosing to NOT do the things God is telling you to do, you are a liar in your profession of faith in God thru Jesus Christ and you are not living the truth. That is not a good place to be. It leads to, or is, eternal separation from God.(1 John)

Reflect on this passage again and reflect on your life. Is your life Christ-like, or is it like the rest of this profane world? Perhaps there is some of each in you, read on. If there is no obedience, no surrender of all, no cost to your life, has His price of the Cross, His surrender to the Father, His obedience been of any value to you? In other words, are you saved?

Many times during these periods God will show us pieces that are not from Him and not helping us become more like Jesus. Instead, these pieces are pulling us apart from Jesus and weaving designs of our own within the masterpiece that He painted. These are pieces we have forced into a slot rather than allowing the Holy Spirit to insert the proper pieces in their correct places. When this happens we must use the power of the Holy Spirit to rip these ill-fitting pieces out and throw them as far away as possible. Let someone else find them for their puzzle. They might then be useful and fulfilling to that someone, where to us they were only detractors and blemishes in the masterpiece that is our life. Most of the time they will be no good for anyone and need to be destroyed, He can do that. He has a big fire. When we use the desert times to realign and cleanse our masterpiece, reflecting on all God has done for us and given us, we allow ourselves to be given much more by the loving God who created us to begin with.

Way back in Chapter 8 we discussed that you put you together using the guiding power of the Holy Spirit. Did you catch in this chapter that it is you who must make the changes where the wrong pieces have been plugged in? Did you catch the leading of the Holy Spirit in determining those pieces to be the wrong ones? Take the time right now to cleanse your picture thru the leading and power of the Holy Spirit. If you don't cleanse your picture you will be stuck in desert emptiness until you do.

Let me give you a reference on the above idea.

James 4:7-10

7 Submit yourselves therefore to God. Resist the devil, and he will flee from you.

8 Draw nigh to God, and he will draw nigh to you. Cleanse your hands, ye sinners; and purify your hearts, ye double minded.

9 Be afflicted, and mourn, and weep: let your laughter be turned to mourning, and your joy to heaviness.

10 Humble yourselves in the sight of the Lord, and he shall lift you up.

Notice that we are told to: submit, resist, draw nigh, cleanse, purify, humble, be and let. All of these are things we must do. We can only do them through the power of His Holy Spirit living within us as a major part of all that we are. Remember those three focal pieces of our puzzle. Without them nothing happens to put us together. Having them, we must do the putting of us together.

In addition to the times of growth or even times of the emptiness of a desert, we will run into seasons of being torn apart, piece by piece. When we are properly serving in our call, God will come along and tear, cut, rip away pieces that are in the way of continuing to grow or serve, much the same as a vineyard tender will prune the vines that bear lots of fruit in order for them to bear even more in the following season. (John 15)

And then there are the times when you just can't find a piece and/or a place that fit together. No openings available to continue building. This does not mean that you are a finished product; it means God is giving you a quiet time in

life in order to prepare for a greater blessing of expansion.
Hang on.

Chapter 14

GIFTS FROM A LOVING FATHER

As part of our Masterpiece Puzzle, we have pieces that are talents and others that are gifts. As we utilize those talents and gifts, we build up other folks.(Ephesians 4:12, 1 Corinthians 12:7) In return other folks use their talents and gifts to build us up.

Talents and gifts do not have the same definition. Talents are given by God to each individual regardless of where they put their faith. We are born with them, if you will. Talents are nurtured through practice, practice, practice, or maybe ignored by taking them for granted or never attempting to expound on them. Talents, or even a lack of talents, can be seen and heard (oh, can they be heard) at the beginner's music and dance recitals. Two six year olds dancing; one falls on his face constantly and the other is poised, graceful and a joy to watch. Watch the Olympics, talents practiced to perfection.

Gifts, on the other hand, spring from God only to benefit the Kingdom of God. Gifts listed in Scripture include tongues, healing, teaching, prophecy, discernment, and many others of a less tangible nature. God bestows gifts on people as needed to benefit the Church, the Body of Christ.(1 Corinthians 12:7) They may be given for a long period of time, such as the career evangelist; or for only a short period, as in the case of touching and healing one individual. All results are for the Glory of God.

Some may have a talent for something like languages (tongues). If so, they will have to work at learning the language and using it, but it will come much easier for them than to one without the talent. If a person receives the gift of language (tongues) from God, it will come on suddenly, for a Godly purpose, and may or may not stay with them.

Talents are used by everyone, usually for the person's benefit, while gifts are used for the Glory of God at His time for the building of His Kingdom (THE BIG PICTURE).(1 Corinthians 12-14)

One of the current side effects of not understanding the difference between gifts and talents is causing an argument within the Church which is bringing disunity among believers. No talent used to God's Glory or gift given for God's people will ever cause disunity in the true Church. The author of 1 Corinthians states that there are factions, divisions, disunity within the Church and that should not be.(1 Corinthians 1:10-11) Ephesians states that unity is key to the Kingdom of God; one in body, Spirit, hope, Lord, faith, baptism, God and Father of all who is above us all, through us all and in us all.(Ephesians 4)

How can God's masterpiece ever be complete, the Masterpiece of THE BIG PICTURE, if there are divisions, schisms, disunity? By the definition of "complete" it would be impossible. To be complete is to be whole. The whole is not divided. The whole can be divided, but then it is not whole. Picture a pie cut in 6 pieces. While in the pan it is whole. As pieces are taken it is divided, each part separate from the other, the pie is not whole. Very soon you have nothing but a dirty dish, which has happened and is happening to many congregations at this present time. Divisions are power struggles, power struggles come from pride, and God hates pride.

There are many places where we can differ in thinking and still focus on the same goal, and this is one of them; the definitions of talents and gifts. I can love you, worship with you and work with you even if I disagree with you on some things, BUT God's list in Ephesians 4 is sacrosanct. When all the believing seekers of pieces can agree on that no matter where they choose to worship or what style of worship or the name over the door, the individuals within the Body of Christ will then be building the masterpieces of themselves into their God given glorious state and be building the Masterpiece of THE BIG PICTURE.

Just remember, we all have talents and we are given gifts by God to the level we need them to perform and fulfill God's purpose to His Glory at that moment in time. Something I heard a while back applies here: The Spirit convicts, God get the Glory and all I have to do is love.

Chapter 16

THE UNPLEASANT PIECES

It will not take long to figure out that there are some pieces we really don't want to have in our puzzle. They may be blue, deep red or even black as a dominant color. These are the pieces of those horrible, no good, very bad, terrible days in our lives. The days of depression or depressing events might be symbolized by blue, the painful days by their blood red color. and the black indication those days of loss of a loved one, either by death or separation of some other type. There will be some pieces the color of suffering mixed in the collection of our pieces. James says to count it all joy when we are called upon to be tested.(James 1:2, Matthew 1:12, Acts 5:41, Hebrews 10:34, 1 Peter 4:13,16) Why would he ever say that? The next verse tells us that these trials of faith are working in us for patience, waiting on God, relying on God.(James 1:3) We are told we need patience in order to live the will of God in order to receive His promises in our lives.(Hebrews 10:36) Not only do those trials build us up in patience, God uses every one of them for the bettering of the Kingdom through us.(Romans 8:28) That's one awesome promise for us to hang onto in those days of pain and suffering.

Take a serious look at your life. See any rough spots, days that were hard to live through or even ones where you may have even wished for your life to be taken? If you are a Christ follower you can probably see something that God taught you through those days. Think about those watching you suffer with resolute strength in Christ. The witness you provide to them may be life changing and you might never even know it. If you are not a follower yet, perhaps you might see something there for you or not.

There was a time in my life when my Mother was dying. Most of us come to that time in life when we lose a parent. Mom was dying of cancer, a twelve year fight. I prayed, oh how I prayed. My faith in God through Jesus Christ was truly tried. Up until that time I had never been able to stay in a hospital for longer than 10 or 15 minutes at a time with long breaks, like days, in between. There was only one stint of me being in a hospital when I was 19 and I got out of there as fast as I could convince the doctor to let me go.

The last weeks of Mom's life on earth she was in a hospital over 250 miles away. Each weekend we would travel to the hospital and visit with Mom and Dad. I stayed all day no matter what my mind was telling me about hospitals. My claustrophobia was strong, but my desire to see Mom was stronger, God had answered my prayers in that regard with the power to stay through the fear of the walls which seemed constantly to be closing in.

The last weekend I saw her alive I spent over 10 hours with her in that room in one day with only one break at midday to go down to the cafeteria. As I left at the end of the day, she called, "Love you, baby." My next hug will be in heaven at the feet of Jesus.

Okay now, why did I tell you that story?

That was the toughest time in my life. Between my love for Mom and the claustrophobia, every day was a battle of trial and faith. I had just started as a pastor of a small church. God knew I wouldn't do well as a pastor without the ability to stay in a hospital with hurting people when the need arose. He used that tough time to teach me I had the strength in me from Him to stick it out no matter what the fear and emotional levels were.

During this whole piece of my life, with the black, blue and red pieces being plugged in right and left, God taught me the lesson I would need. As hard as it is to say, I needed that lesson and He taught me in a powerful way. Mom was 70. She had a good life except for having to raise me. She prayed for me for 49 years. She taught me all the hard lessons of life. I didn't enjoy many of the lessons, but I surely did need to learn of God's lessons for me. Mom's life was a gift to me and her death, as rough as it was, was also. It was going to happen someday, so God used that opportunity for His glory and my benefit.

Have you ever felt the presence of God in a hospital room?

Chapter 16

OUR RESPONSIBILITY

It doesn't take us long to realize that with all this building of us by God inspired and/or directed experiences that we have some responsibilities.

God gave me the gift of being able to stay in a hospital room for hours. What could happen if I didn't use that gift in the ministry God has given me? I would not be comforting those who are in the hospital. I would not be helping those who are in the waiting room as loved ones go through surgery and procedures, mild to dangerous. Just think of the doctor doing those procedures. If he did not use his God given talents to assist God in healing, many would not have the quality of life they now have and many would die from simple injuries or major diseases.

God has given many the gift of evangelism. If Billy Graham and others had not used those gifts to the glory of God just think of the millions who would not have heard of the saving Grace of our loving God. The story goes around that if Dwight had not witnessed to Billy, or Billy had not witnessed to Jim, or Jim had not witnessed Larry, Larry had not witnessed to Sue, or Sue had not used her gift to teach that Sunday School class to Mary, or Mary had not prayed for her son, Bob, and Bob had not been your youth leader who witnessed to you, you would have never met Jesus.

Farfetched?

Think about it.

All it takes is one person failing to use their God given talents and gifts to His Glory and who knows how many will die without the knowledge of God's amazing Grace. The pile of the pieces to unfinished masterpieces will be large enough even with us using the gifts God has given us to His glory.

How about those who use those talents for their own gain? Think how you could poison the work of the Lord by thinking only of your own benefit. Think of Jim Bakker. The scandal around his use of funds donated to his ministry was even more harmful to the Kingdom of God than his sexual sin in my opinion. It set back donations to faithful, truthful, and honest ministries for years and I am not sure they are as good as they could be today because of that one ministry's indiscretions.

What about Jim Jones? He worked hard for the Lord and let it go to his head and he became obsessed with the idea of his own god-ship. The debacle and massacre at Jonestown was the result. This was just another cult that led people astray; and in this case to literal death.

What about the sexual sin of so many pastors and priests? - A scandal of the highest order. My heart cries and sometimes even my eyes cry when I hear of those pastors, priests and even *"Christian"* entertainers falling into sexual sin.

Over and over we have seen on the front page of the local media the results of people using their talents and even gifts to their own benefit and not the glory of God. The effect of these is the degradation of the Glory of God in the eyes of those who do not know the real God. Sloppy or phony "Christians" do more harm to THE BIG PICTURE than Satan and all his demons. This is exactly the reason God judged Israel so harshly at the time of the captivity to Assyria and then Babylon. They degraded God by worshipping other gods, idols. Anything that is more important than God in your life is an idol. Get rid of it. NOW!

God's forgiving love is still available to each of us who

stumble or fall into whatever sin is handy through that same repentance and forgiveness we discussed in Chapter 9. Repentance becomes our lifeline to restoration, our bridge to beauty.

BUT!!!!! Grace is not an excuse to sin or permission to sin, (Romans 6:1-2) it is the power to be free of sin.(Romans 6:14-18)

Chapter 17

BRIDGES TO BEAUTY

As we watch we find that these horrible, no good, very bad, terrible times in our lives become bridges to beauty. Each of them becomes a link to new experiences and opportunities to use our gifts to the glory of God as we continue to see the masterpiece that is us come together. Each and every experience in our life is an experience to grow, expanding His masterpiece and becoming all He wants us to be.

The Bible tells us that God uses all things in our lives for good if we love Him and are called by Him to His work.(Romans 8:28) Just think, all of those terrible days and experiences are just opportunities and training for greater service and joy in the Lord's viewpoint when we are aligned by God's Grace out of our sins.

God has used the horror stories of my sin and weaknesses to His glory in every day of my ministry. I don't understand it, but I really am awed by how God can do that, which is also no excuse or invitation to continue in sin or start new ones. Every counselor I have ever worked with has become a counselor because of his/her own struggles. The drug and alcohol counselors have all been either junkies or alkies, or had to live with one they really cared about. The same goes for those who deal with mental issues. What has torn us up or brought us down drives a desire to help others out of or through similar issues in their life.

When we look at those days through His eyes we can see the service and feel the joy that being His masterpiece leads us to. We know the fabulous privilege of being a servant of the King of kings. Then again, Jesus tells us we are not servants, but friends; friends working together with Him for a common goal – the Kingdom of God.(John 15:14-21)

The Bible tells us also that since we are His we will suffer.(Romans 8:17, 1 Corinthians 4:12, Philippians 3:10, John 15:20-27) It also tells us that those that God loves (which is everybody), He disciplines, He chastises.(2 Chronicles 7:13, Hebrews 12:5) After all, He is our loving Heavenly Father and what father who loves his children would not discipline them according to the severity of their misdeeds in order to bring them through the problem, into forgiveness and a change of heart/behavior?

God goes a step beyond. He brings us through trials in our lives purposefully to grow our faith in Him. He promises never to give us a trial we cannot handle in Him.(1 Corinthians 10:13) He also promises that we should count in all joy, as if it were a great thing to happen, when we are called upon to suffer many different trials.(James 1:3)

Now why would He say that? The simplest human answer is He has found us strong and wishes to grow that strength. Faith is like a muscle. It must be worked to grow. If we don't use it, faith atrophies and dies. Remember that James tells us that inactive faith is dead faith. If our faith is dead so are we.(James 2:17-18) Only in trial and effort do we grow our faith. Those horrible, no good, very bad days are the trials He uses to grow that faith.

My son's football coach was always giving out little wisdoms like, "No pain, no gain" and "You gotta want it." God uses our pain to confirm our want. If there is no pain in our growth, there is no desire for God, consequently no gain. We must also remember that the sufferings of today are nothing when compared to the glory we shall see and receive when our masterpiece is complete in the presence of the

Artist.(Romans 8:18)

In looking at all these ideas we come to the conclusion that the horrible, no good, very bad, terrible days are a bridge to a blessing which may or may not be discerned for a long time. In each of these days we will grow in faith and service to the Maker of our masterpiece.

Just think on the last horrible, no good, very bad day we will ever see; the day we die. In that day we will go from suffering to perfection of peace and joy in the wink of an eye. Our greatest darkness, death, is conquered in Christ to become our greatest transition from death into life everlasting. In that moment we will understand it all. Then our masterpiece will be complete.(2 Timothy 1:12)

Chapter 18

FRUIT

For now we see the proverbial masterpiece of the simple still life painting of three or four pieces of fruit, heavily shadowed, sometimes among other food items on a table forming in our own minds. You know the one, every art student has to paint over and over again in order to learn shading, detail and view perspective.

We talked of gifts in a previous chapter. Gifts are wonderful. Gifts are always exciting, even when it is a garish, sequined tie from Aunt Suzie. When we as humans grow something, the satisfaction with that growth is its living and the fruit it bears. It may be a tree that provides shade or apples after years of careful nurturing, or it may be the milk, wool, meat, leather, etc, provided after constant care.

God feels the same way after carefully stroking gifts into us as He paints. He strokes. He watches. He nurtures. He watches. He guides. His satisfaction comes when He gathers the fruit that has been produced in us through the indwelling of the Holy Spirit.(1 Corinthians 3)

This fruit is not the miraculous extensions of the Holy Spirit so that we may carry out the tasks painted into our masterpiece, they are internal gifts that make us shine into a dark and dreary, dying world for Him. The Bible calls them, "The Fruit of the Spirit."(Galatians 5:22-23) These fruits are:

Love

Joy

Peace

Patience

Kindness

Goodness

Faithfulness

Gentleness

Self-control

When we look at this list, we see much that is to be desired from just a human perspective, let alone from a God perspective.

Look at each one. What would it be like if you and all your friends lived these attributes in your day to day activities? What would it be like if the whole community you live in lived these characteristics? How about your nation? Or, the whole world?

Just think of the resources that would be freed up when all these were applied in the lives of this world. No more courts. No more defense departments. No more police. No more need for expensive systems of government, a simple benevolent entity to be in charge and I am not even sure that would be required if we all lived out these fruit to the maximum extent in our lives. Talk about Utopia! It will happen, but that's another story or as Paul Harvey said, "The rest of the story."

The Golden Rule says we are to treat others as we would like to be treated.(Matthew 7:12) These fruit would make that the norm. The Ten Commandments (Exodus 20) and all of the Sermon on the Mount (Matthew 5-7) point to the idea presented here. When Jesus was challenged by the Pharisees (the overbearing, self-privileged politicians of His day) concerning the greatest commandment (law), Jesus responded with, "Love God with all you are. But wait, we cannot separate this from the second greatest, which is Love everybody else." (my paraphrase)(Matthew 22:29-30) So, the simplicity of the fruit is that we are carrying out the greatest commandment and the second greatest, the two being inseparable.

Many places and religions teach us that we must be a servant to others, but there is usually a catch to that idea. Most believe that through being a servant we attain to some high result, but the masterpiece of God that we are shows us doing these things as a result of His artistry rather than to cause it. The works in His masterpiece are seen through our faith and as a result of His Grace; therefore they come out of faith and Grace, not into it.(Ephesians 2:8-10, James 2:14-26) In other words, you cannot work your way into Grace, only faith gets you there.

All these individual fruit of the Spirit working in us have a very distinct purpose to facilitate in us. That purpose can be seen in the purpose of the Holy Spirit. If you remember, the Holy Spirit is the power to get the Masterpiece completed according to God's plan. Each of the fruit is the Holy Spirit working in us. He brings us to the point where through faith and the indwelling of the Spirit, we can truly love. Really love to the place where we care more about others than ourselves. Not just lust, desire, be attracted to, or want to be with for what you can gain from them, but truly unconditional love.

At this point I will make a defining statement and you can quote me anytime you would like to, "Without the Holy Spirit of God dwelling in you through faith that Jesus Christ is all the Word says He is, you do not know what love really is."

In defense of that statement we have the Bible, the Word of God. The Word tells us God is love. Not a love, not an example of love, but, love – plain and simple. So, without Him there is no love. We can redefine it all we want, but the truth still remains that He and He alone is love. Nothing else is love. Not sacrifice. Not sex. Not even chocolates and flowers. You can base getting yourself together on many things, but the happiness and completeness you want is elusive and is never found in the ideas of this world. When God's love is the base, all is in its proper place and you are right where you should be with your Creator; serving Him in your own unique way of using His love to love others. In order to know and have love, you must have Him.

Look at the list of the gifts again and you will see that each of the gifts of the Holy Spirit is a powerful discipline, all of which are extremely difficult, even impossible, for the human to perform without tremendous power and concentration. Collecting all nine together and doing the math of nine times impossible or extremely difficult equals unequivocally improbable to the nth degree. Only the power of God the Holy Spirit can make this possible. He is the control factor that makes the improbable and impossible task simply accomplished by quitting our own efforts and surrendering to the will of God which makes us all that He painted us to be.

You.

Chapter 19

THE VIEW FROM THE CANVAS

We have seen that the greatest commandment is "Love God," followed by the inseparable "love everyone else." Our masterpiece itself points directly to that greatest of commandments.

First, it is painted by Him as an act of love. He sent His Son to die for our sins as an act of love. He has done all He can do to draw us to Him as an act of Love. He is preparing a place for the Masterpiece that is us to live for all eternity in His presence as an act of love. We could go and on with the acts of love God has performed for us. He made us to return that love.

Second, the greatest of these is seen in our masterpiece itself. It is in the image of His only Son. How much more love can be expressed than to be created to look like a child of the Father?

Now, picture the brag wall in any grandparent's home. As you look at the pictures of the children and grandkids isn't there a sense of familiarity in each one and in all of them collectively? Each is made from a blend of the genes of the parents, grandparents, and great-grandparents, etc, etc, etc.

Now picture again your masterpiece on the Father's wall. You have only one spiritual parent, the Father; one set of spiritual genes, you are part of the family. Your masterpiece is hanging on His brag wall with His genes just as His Son, Jesus, has.

He asks you to live as a respected, loved, important part of the family. He asks you to love as He loves you. Love Him. The Son says, "If you love me, keep my commandments." Love everyone else. "Love your neighbor as yourself."

Go again to the wall and check out your picture. You see a will. You know that you can feel, taste, hear, see, smell, emote, think, move, and many other attributes, all from the Father.

Did you notice anything else? Perhaps you need to study it more. Take your time. Yeah, you see hair color and style, expression, build, all that, but look some more. Do not look at the details, that could take the rest of your life. Look at the picture as a whole. One major feature stands out in my mind which is extremely important.

You are facing the viewers, outward.

Why do you suppose that is? Other than no one takes a picture of someone from the back to hang on the brag wall. We take pictures for the brag wall to show off the physical attributes of our descendants.

You are facing outward so your focus can be outward just as Christ's was. Your will needs to be outward. Your senses need to be fine-tuned outward. We do not focus outward for self-preservation. It is the Father's task to preserve us. We do not face outward to find what might be out there for ourselves, which is sin (coveting, selfishness, and all other types of MEisms). All of our attributes are to be intent upon what is outside of self so that you may love all others as the Father loves you. You are better able to see the needs of others when looking at them and not at yourself. You cannot see what is behind you. Although, I swear my mother could.

Through a total understanding of this outward focus of your masterpiece you develop the same focus as the Father and the Son which brings you to a total love of others, a caring, concerned, THEY focus which is the total, complete dying to self simply stated, "Love others as you love yourself."

In loving God, we come to faith and an appreciation of all He has done for us. In loving God, we come to a desire to serve, and our service is loving others using the example of His love for us. His love flows into us like a cold drink on a hot day until we are filled to the brim, packed down, and overflowing with it. That overflow is us reaching out to others because of and with His love.

Love is so important that Jesus stated the most important law was, "Love God," the second was so closely tied it was inseparable, "Love everybody else like you love yourself." Inferred in these two rules is the idea that loving God is a total surrender of all we are to God. In doing so we become all He created us to be. We are then in total satisfaction with self, which allows us to love all others without the tripping over the stones of competition and pride that just get in the way.

In other words, only in God are we capable of loving because we then understand the depths of what love really is. Because we now understand what love really is, our outlook is outward to the needs of others.

Chapter 20

WATCH OUT!

Now is the time to really be careful. Two things move to get in our way and keep us from finishing our masterpiece under the guidance of God's Holy Spirit. The first is a simple one. As a cartoon critter once said, "We have met the enemy and he is us." We begin to get in our own way. Pride kicks in. "Lookie what I have done," becomes our thought. "I am so wonderfully beautiful." Ad nauseam. Thomas a' Kempus once said, "Who has a greater struggle than those who labor to overcome themselves." Wise man, huh? Nobody wins when we struggle against ourselves. I am as strong as me and me fighting me just tires me out. Therefore, I make solemn request of the Father in Jesus' name to take charge of the battle and whup me into shape so I can continue with the masterpiece HE has created for me.

The second is much more obscure and devious, SATAN. Satan usually moves in the ideas of the world presented to us through every one of the five senses we may have. Look at Peter, at the Last Supper of Christ with His Disciples, Jesus told Peter Satan wished to sift him.(Luke 22:31) To sift is to press or draw it through a strainer. Have you ever felt like you were being drawn or pressed through a strainer? The world throws out so many ideas that are totally unbeneficial to our masterpiece that we must strain it all through the filter of God's Word and His righteousness. In other words, how HE would do it.

We get strained and sifted as we search for our pieces. We see one just lying there and it seems to say to us, "Try me, you will like me. I will make you feel real good. I am what you need. I am just what you have been looking for. I will solve all your problems. Choose me. CHOOSE ME!" Satan does nothing new. He is the father of lies.(John 8:44) He is a murderer.(ibid) But, he is powerful. He is beautiful in a worldly way. He makes deals for the hearts of mankind. Let's look at the temptation of Eve again.

Genesis 3:1-7
1 Now the serpent was more subtil than any beast of the field which the LORD God had made. And he said unto the woman, Yea, hath God said, Ye shall not eat of every tree of the garden?
2 And the woman said unto the serpent, We may eat of the fruit of the trees of the garden:
3 But of the fruit of the tree which is in the midst of the garden, God hath said, Ye shall not eat of it, neither shall ye touch it, lest ye die.
4 And the serpent said unto the woman, Ye shall not surely die:
5 For God doth know that in the day ye eat thereof, then your eyes shall be opened, and ye shall be as gods, knowing good and evil.
6 And when the woman saw that the tree was good for food, and that it was pleasant to the eyes, and a tree to be desired to make one wise, she took of the fruit thereof, and did eat, and gave also unto her husband with her; and he did eat.
7 And the eyes of them both were opened, and they knew that they were naked; and they sewed fig leaves together, and made themselves aprons.

Remember this? No? Reread the first chapter.

Eve thought she was right on the money with God. She even added to His spoken rule and made it even tougher on herself. Satan twisted the entire truth of the situation around and convinced Eve that God was a liar. By throwing the same words back at Eve that God had given Eve only using them in a different context, physical death versus spiritual death, he convinced Eve to chow down and to assist the only other person (Adam) on earth to do the same.

Eve allowed Satan a foothold in her life by just talking with him. The real gap in her walk with God was when she tried to reason/argue with Satan. He twisted her words, smiled pretty, and she succumbed. Can any of us say truthfully that we are wiser than Eve and Adam? Not. Do not allow Satan a foothold in your life in any way, shape, or form. Any time a believer falls into the simplest of sins which disconnect them from God, Satan has a toehold and he will be quick to shove his entire foot into that toehold unless we follow simple directions which God has given us.

The one thing that holds our masterpiece together no matter how we fail or how much Satan tries to get us to fail is GRACE.(Ephesians 2:8-19) Grace is the glue that continues to hold us together at the very core of our being. No matter how hard Satan tries he cannot defeat Grace.

We exercise Grace through the simplicity of prayer, Bible reading, and focusing on Christ without lives. When Satan does trip us up or we get proud, we simply go to Christ in sincere repentance and He is more that willing to forgive us our sins.(1 John 1:9)

To continue the caution of this chapter let me say this, any time there is a burst of construction on your masterpiece, any time you feel God working strongly through you, any time you are really feeling good about what God is doing with you, those are the times to really be careful and strongly focus on God. Satan will surely be on the attack one way or another to stop you from growing and bringing the ministry (service) you are doing which is bearing fruit to an end. He cannot stand the success of God's people. He must destroy their work, effort and testimony.

Chapter 21

THE BEGINNING

Now YOU know everything I know about the puzzle of Theology as it relates to our walk with God. It is time to start or move forward confidently toward all God painted you to be. Complete this masterpiece that is YOU to His Glory.

Too often we look at salvation as our ticket out of Hell and nothing more. But, salvation is not about US, it is about HIM. HE created us. HE gave us HIS expectations. HE provided the opportunity to walk with HIM through HIS dying on the cross of Calvary and HIS resurrection. HE calls us to HIM. HE provides the power to get it all done with the power of HIS Holy Spirit. HE guides all the way. HE gets the glory.

HE states in HIS Word that HE will keep all HIS promises no matter what for HIS Holy Name's sake and only for HIS name's sake.(Ezekiel 36:21-34) HE goes on to say that HE will cleanse us and put HIS Spirit within us.(Ezekiel 36:25-38)

You see, it is all about HIM. HE uses us for HIS works on this world.

Matthew 5:16 personalized - Let my works so shine before men that they will see my good works and give God the glory.

A personal passage I keep posted so I can remember it day to day.

I just have to throw one more item in here, if you haven't caught on through all the preceding pages; you make your masterpiece by assisting others in making their masterpiece. You complete you by being a servant to them. Once God becomes the center of your life, you are used to complete all the other masterpieces, while all the other masterpieces are being used to complete the masterpiece that is you. It is no longer as Jesus said, "Come and see" to the disciples, it becomes dying to self and serving others with your life as He showed them and said, "Go and tell", which might also be stated, "Go and show."

Does that make sense?

It is fantasmagorically powerful when you realize that when you become HIS servant to others, all those others becomes HIS servants to you. Think on that. You serve a few hundred people, while at the same time that few hundred people serve you, and through that you become complete, fulfilled, His masterpiece.

That's HIS plan.

Ask HIM to plug HIMSELF into the middle of you and get going for HIS glory.

End

If you liked this book, let Doug know at
writingsailor@gmail.com.
Thank you for reading my small work for God.
May you be blessed.
doug

Doug earned his Doctor of Ministry from Andersonville Theological Seminary after doing whatever it took to graduate from high school, survive 20 years in the U.S. Navy, flunk out of UNM, earn a BA in education from Ottawa University, live through 8 years of middle school teaching, and 27 years of pastoring. He spends his spare time watching the weeds grow on his ranch in rural Arizona where he lives with his wife of 43 years and three dogs, with occasional visits from their grandkids and six adult children.